ATLANTIC STUDIES ON SOCIETY IN CHANGE

NO. 68

Editor-in-Chief, Béla K. Király
Associate Editor-in-Chief, Peter Pastor
Assistant Editor, Edit Völgyesi

In Memory of

JÁNOS DECSY

(1928-1993)

The Hungarian Minority's Situation in Ceausescu's Romania

Rudolf Joó, Editor
Andrew Ludanyi, Revising Editor

Translated from Hungarian by
Chris Tennant

Social Science Monographs, Boulder, Colorado
Atlantic Research and Publications, Inc.
Highland Lakes, New Jersey

Distributed by Columbia University Press, New York
1994

EAST EUROPEAN MONOGRAPHS, NO. CCCLXXIII

Copyright © 1994
by Atlantic Research and Publications, Inc.

Library of Congress Catalog Card Number 94-70045
ISBN 0-88033-270-0

Printed in the United States of America

Table of Contents

List of Tables		vii
Preface to the Series		ix
Foreword		xi
Preface to the Original Edition		xv
Introduction		1
Chapter I	Preliminary Observations	17
Chapter II	Historical Considerations	21
Chapter III	The Population Profile of the Hungarians in Romania	27
Chapter IV	The Political and Legal Status of the National Minorities	39
Chapter V	Minority Access to Media, Education, and Culture	59
Chapter VI	Church-State Relations and Minority Existence	79
Chapter VII	Hungary and the Hungarians of Romania	91
Chapter VIII	Emigrants, Immigrants, and Refugees	101
Chronology		109
Endnotes		121
Documents		133
Name Index		145
Place Index		147
Volumes Published in "Atlantic Studies on Society in Change"		151

List of Tables

1. Distribution of the Romanian Population by Ethnic Group and Mother Tongue (censuses of 1948-1977) — 29
2. Estimates of the Number of Hungarians in Romania by Major Hungarian-Inhabited Areas (1977 and 1987) — 31
3. The Number of Hungarians in Romania as Estimated on the Basis of Religious Affiliation (1987) — 32
4. The Population of Transylvania by Ethnic Groups and Linguistic Affiliation (official census data in thousands) — 68
5. Changes in the Hungarian Population of Eight Major Transylvanian Cities (official census data) — 69
6. Instruction in Hungarian for Primary-Level Pupils (Grades 1-8) — 70
7. Instruction in Hungarian for Students of Secondary Schools — 70
8. Ethnic Composition of the Teaching Staff at the University of Cluj-Napoca (1970/71 - 1980/81) — 72
9. Ethnic Composition of the Teaching Staff at the Institute of Medicine and Pharmacology of Tîrgu Mureş (1970/71 and 1982/83) — 72

Preface to the Series

The present volume is a component of a series that, when completed will constitute a comprehensive survey of the many aspects of East European society.

The books in the series deal with the peoples whose homelands lie between the Germans to the west, the Russians to the east and the Mediterranean and Adriatic seas to the south. They constitute a particular civilization, one that is at once an integral part of Europe, yet substantially different from the West. The area is characterized by a rich variety in language, religion, and government. The study of this complex area demands a multidisciplinary approach and, accordingly, our contributors to the series represent several academic disciplines. They have been drawn from the universities and other scholarly institutions in the United States and Western Europe, as well as East and Central Europe. The editors of the present volume are distinguished scholars. At the present Dr. Rudolf Joó is State Secretary at the Hungarian Ministry of Defense, and Dr. Andrew Ludanyi is Professor of Political Science at Ohio Northern University.

The editors, of course, take full responsibility for ensuring the comprehensiveness, cohesion, internal balance, and scholarly quality of the series. We cheerfully accept this responsibility and intend this work to be neither a justification nor condemnation of the policies, attitudes, and activities of any persons involved. At the same time, because the contributors represent so many different disciplines, interpretations, and schools of thought, our policy in this, as in the past and future volumes, is to present their contributions without major modifications.

Foreword

Atlantic Research and Publications has selected to publish a re-worked version of *Report on the Situation of the Hungarian Minority in Rumania*. This work was printed in Budapest in 1988 under the aegis of the Hungarian Democratic Forum. Two major reasons account for this selection: First, that the *Report* is in itself a historic document. It is the result of the healthy national self-assertion of a non-governmental organization (Democratic Forum) challenging the official policies of Hungary's Kádár administration which ignored the plight of Hungarian minorities in neighboring states. On the nationalities question this is the first time that a non-governmental organization publicly challenged an East European autocracy's right to make policy. In Poland Solidarity, in Czechoslovakia Charta 77, were the only other instances of such challenges, but these did not extend to policies on the fate of ethnic and national minorities.

The second reason for this selection is that it is an excellent summary of the status of the Hungarian minority in Romania under the Ceausescu dictatorship. Such brief but well-documented treatments are woefully lacking in the English-speaking world on a problem area that is becoming more and more central to the peace and stability of the region. The "Report" also presents a balanced analysis that rises above the strident nationalism of the Ceausescu-dominated variety.

A third reason may also be added to above major two considerations. Just a little more than a year after the publication of the *Report*, the Ceausescu administration was overthrown at the end of December, 1989. Ironically, this momentous change did not bring about a total rejection of the Ceausescu legacy. Particularly in the area of minority policies, the ghost of the former dictator is alive and well. The current Romanian leadership seems to follow in his footsteps in scapegoating and persecuting the Hungarian minority. To understand these policies, the outline of the Ceausescu past is most enlightening.

The republication of the *Report* under the new title of *The Hungarian Minority's Situation in Ceausescu's Romania* requires some additional observations. The re-edited version makes the issues of interethnic relations in Romania clearer for those readers who are unfamiliar with the history of the region and its peoples. This has been accomplished with the addition of some explanatory footnotes as well as a brief historical chronology. The style has also been re-worked to provide more unity and clarity. While the content remains the same, it is at least stylistically a new book.

One important change, however, in both the title and the book is the spelling of Romania. While the original *Report* spelled the name of "Rumania" with "u", in the present version we have adopted the now accepted practice of spelling the name with an "o". Since 1990 even *The New York Times* has made this switch from "Ru" to the Ceausescu instituted "Ro". While we too now use the designation Romania, we wish to stress that the previously used spelling was more in line with both the actual pronunciation of the name and the history of the designation. The French spelling reflects this even today as Roumanie.

Ceausescu changed the spelling to Romania not much to designate independence from Moscow or from Slavic roots, but to emphasize the "Roman" origins of the "Rumanians". This is all linked to the revival of exclusivist nationalism among the Romanians which Ceausescu had attempted to use to distract attention from the shortcomings of his own leadership. However, he was also reacting against the historical implications of the "Rumanian" designation. Since Romania only came into being as a unified state in 1859, prior to that time "its" territories were called Wallachia and Moldavia (which after World War I were expanded with the additions of Bessarabia, Bukovina, Transylvania and Dobrogea). The majority inhabitants in these provinces referred to themselves as Rumîn (sing.) or Rumîni (pl.). The most likely and plausible explanation for this is that as vassals of the Ottoman Turkish Empire, and as Vlach subjects of the Empire's Balkan territories from the end of the 14th to the middle of the 19th century, they accepted the overlord Turkish designation for them. The Turks called their conquered subjects of the former Byzantine Empire the inhabitants of "Rum" or "Rumelia" (the latter became the official provincial designation of the future Bulgaria for a time). In other words, the Turks referred to their conquest on the European side of the Dardanel'es and Bosporus as Rumelia, while they referred to the regions on the Asian side as Anatolia. In this way they too claimed to be successors of the Roman Empire, via state succession, and via maintenance of continuity in the designation of the territories they annexed to their expanded empire. Its a minor point to note that their succession was to the Eastern

Roman Empire, which for centuries had already been Greek in culture, religion, and language. Of course the more obvious and direct linkages are frequently ignored, when the symbolism of "Roman" means grandeur and glory, something that of course Ceausescu's Romania was not.

Finally, the editors wish to thank all those individuals who contributed to the original "Report". It was originally produced by the efforts of a team of scholars, some contributing entire chapters, some others just parts of chapters or important data. At the time, the entire work was done illegally and some of the contributors used pen-names to hide their identity. Herewith, the editors of the present volume wish to acknowledge the debt they owe to this original team which included Attila Ara-Kovács, György Dávid, Rudolf Joó, Géza Entz, József Nagy, Károly Antal Tóth, and Judit Vásárhelyi. They also wish to thank Júlia Balogh, Zoltán Bíró, Lajos Für, László Hámos, Béla K. Király, Peter Pastor, Géza Szőcs, Gáspár Miklós Tamás, Árpád E. Varga and many unnamed others who made the *Report* and its original English translation possible. For the re-worked version of the *Report* the revising editor is particularly indebted to Mrs. Barbara Roberts for her patience and quality wordprocessing skills.

Andrew Ludanyi

Preface to the Original Edition

At the first meeting of the Hungarian Democratic Forum, held at Lakitelek on September 27, 1987, it was proposed that the fate of the Hungarian minorities living beyond the country's borders should be placed at the top of its agenda. The condition of these minorities, which has received some publicity in the international press, has deteriorated to an alarming degree. This fact and the continued persistent indifference of official Hungarian circles over the decades, has prompted the Hungarian Democratic Forum to adopt the Lakitelek proposal and to undertake the task of preparing an up to date analysis of the situation.

This did not come about by chance. Many of the Forum organizers and the participants of the Lakitelek meeting had for many years been personally committed and involved with this matter. They had raised the issue on numerous occasions. These same individuals had repeatedly attempted to draw the attention of the national leadership and the public to the impending dangers and the irreparable consequences involved. Unfortunately, they were unsuccessful in dispelling the indifference or in promoting a better comprehension of the situation. The shortsightedness of the official leadership prevailed. History will hold these leaders accountable for their willful neglect and dereliction of responsibility. They have jeopardized the fate of those Hungarians who, through no fault of their own, had been reduced to the status of minority citizens in the neighboring countries.

This decision of the Hungarian Democratic Forum was followed immediately by preparations for a conference. First we had to do a thorough assessment of the issues. Our examination of the facts would have to bring to light the circumstances under which the Hungarian minorities exist in the Carpathian basin.

Apart from a very cautious and unpublished survey conducted in 1971-73 on the cultural and educational situation of the Hungarian minorities, until recently their status was ignored. For some 40 years no comprehensive attempt had been made in Hungary to examine the status of the 3.5 million Hungarians living in neighboring states, of whom more than two million are concentrated in Transylvania. Even less had been done in the neighboring states in the way of data collection or analysis concerning their Hungarian minorities. It seemed as if a conspiracy of silence intended to blot out Hungarian consciousness in both Hungary and the neighboring states. It wanted to eradicate any sense of unity between the Hungarians of Eastern Europe.

This orchestrated national amnesia made it absolutely indispensable that a professional and factual report should be written to fill the void. To this end a conference was the first step. It would focus the attention of both domestic and foreign policy makers on this previously neglected issue. It would also inform the relevant social organizations, potential support groups and the general public. However, because the largest, most historically and culturally significant, Hungarian minority is located in Transylvania and is fighting for its very existence, the Hungarian Democratic Forum decided to first focus attention on this particular group.

The Hungarian Democratic Forum has been able to enlist the know-how of the researchers who are most acquainted with the issue. It was able to recruit Rudolf Joó, a political scientist, who is a well-known authority on minority matters, to assume responsibility for guiding the work of the assembled task force. At the behest of the Hungarian Democratic Forum, some of the country's most distinguished scholars in various fields, 35-40 individuals were called together in February, 1988. Their purpose was to review the situation-analysis prepared by the seven-member task force. The analysis dealt with both basic overall questions and more detailed aspects of the situation. On the basis of this critical review and suggestions for modifications and supplements, the Hungarian Democratic Forum issued a report at the Jurta Theatre on March 6th, 1988. Rudolf Joó presented the essential points of the long report for the assembled delegates.

The fate of Hungarians in Romania is a passion-arousing issue. Thus, the discussions held on the March 6th, attended by more than 700 of Hungary's leading intellectuals, could not satisfy the audience and had to be continued on March 21st. On the basis of the views, recommendations, and new data presented at these sessions, the task force refined and supplemented the analysis. The result is the published final version of the report as presented in this volume. The tragic conclusions of the report are substantiated by the data provided in the text and by the selected documents.

Two versions of the report were prepared: the present full-length version, complete with documents, and a shorter, 37-page summary version. The summary report was initially released at a press conference held on April 25th, 1988. This meeting was covered only by representatives of the independent, non-official publications and not the official Hungarian media. Their attention was focused elsewhere on the Party Conference of May 1988, at which major leaders of the Kádár era were being replaced. Consequently, it is not surprising that the official Hungarian media remained silent concerning this vitally important issue, in line with its past traditions. Nevertheless, the international press provided the report with wider coverage and gave it a favorable reception.

The summary form of the report has been released in both Hungarian and English language editions. The Hungarian edition was sent to leading government and Party functionaries, to the former secretary-general of the Patriotic People's Front, to the presidium of the Hungarian Academy of Sciences, to higher-level members of the Cultural Ministry and the Ministry of Foreign Affairs, and to the head of the interdepartmental commission for Transylvanian refugee affairs, as well as to Hungarian church leaders.

The English edition was also widely distributed. The representatives of foreign public information forums, of course, received the report. Copies, accompanied by separate cover letters, were also sent to the American, British, French, West German, and Swedish government leaders, to the secretary-generals of the Soviet, Chinese, and Italian Communist Parties, to the responsible representatives of the European Parliament and European Council, to the Vatican, as well as to the World Alliance of Reformed Churches, the Jewish Congress, the International Red Cross, responsible subcommittees of the United Nations, and to members of both houses of the U.S. Congress. Some of the latter have already taken a stand on the Hungarian minority issue! And last, but not least, the English edition of the report was sent to those international researchers and scholars who deal with issues pertaining to European ethnic minorities. Subsequent letters, commentaries, and other responses bear witness to the positive reception of the report, akin to its treatment in the international press.

We are aware that history customarily, if not always, verifies, weighs, and judges events and their impact *a posteriori*. However, witnessing the fate of the Hungarian minority in Romania as it plummets towards disaster, we can only hope that the efforts of the Hungarian Democratic Forum will not be in vain. Its work to inform and disseminate data regarding the

Hungarians of Romania may be viewed as the first conscious effort undertaken to avoid disaster in Transylvania. Hopefully, by broadening its appeal and aligning itself with other groups it will be able to help avert the social and cultural dissolution of the communities there. The Hungarian Democratic Forum and the participants of the Jurta Theatre discussions for this reason, insist on: (a) the halting and abandonment of the barbaric plans aimed at destroying thousands of villages in Romania; (b) the elimination of all those conditions which compel minorities to flee the country; (c) the unrestricted right to use minority languages; (d) the guarantee of individual and collective rights; and, (e) the right to autonomy and self-determination. Sensing our historical responsibility, we hope that our shouldered initiatives and activities in this area will not have been in vain.

In closing, we would like to express our gratitude to Chris Tennant, a social scientist and former U.N. planning official, who not only served as translator and editor in the preparation of the English editions of this report but also provided valuable input by way of critical comments and suggestions.

Lajos Für
Professor of History and
Presidium Member of the
Hungarian Democratic Forum

Introduction

After leaving Romania, the Western visitor – or the Western reader who has read reports on the conditions that prevail in Romania – generally expresses disbelief and shock. Shock that conditions such as these are still possible in Europe today and disbelief that these conditions can be tolerated. More precisely, why does a society tolerate such conditions? Particularly, when even in the eastern half of Europe, one after the other less inhuman and brutal systems are collapsing?

Since the present volume and many recently produced studies deal with the conditions, my concern in this introduction will be to explain why it is possible that Romania is still what it is today. Thus, I will not devote my time to the types or the methods of political, psychological, economic and national oppression, nor on the power structure of the present Romania. Instead, I will seek the answer to what makes these overcentralized, surveillance-obsessed totalitarian systems so self-sustaining? Why and until when do we have to wait for a successful challenge to the accumulated contradictions that characterize this system? As we will see, the nationality problem, the fate of the Hungarians in Romania, and the relations between the two peoples, is only seemingly unrelated to this question.

In each society the relationship between the distribution of goods produced, the standard of living of the inhabitants and the control mechanisms of the political order depend on the level of development present at a given time.

Where the largest share of the goods produced is returned to society to satisfy consumer needs, there you will have higher standards of living. At the same time, there will be fewer social conflicts which can threaten either the stability of the order or the economic system. In this kind of society the power structure – which does not resolve conflicts, but simply stifles them – is weak and underdeveloped.

As opposed to this, in societies where the largest share of the produced goods is used to beef-up the power structure, there the standard of living falls and social conflicts grow. The guardians of order must be provided for, and the growth of their numbers automatically reduces the size of the productive workforce. Only rarely are the guardians imported, but invariably the more guards you have, the less will be the number of the real workers.

At any rate, declining standards of living produce social tensions and conflicts. In order to cope with these stresses and insure the system's stability, the apparatus of cooptation and repression is constantly given more and more responsibilities. This begins a vicious cycle whereby the more you manipulate, the more you have to discipline and monitor, the more energy and social goods are consumed by the control system itself.

The linkage between declining living standards and the State control apparatus' insatiable appetite for society's goods, does not lead to appreciable differences in the stability of the system. It does not change, because now a new mechanism controls it, not public satisfaction, but public insecurity and fear. In the instances where conflict becomes uncontrollable, however, and the mechanisms of repression react slowly, or they are weak, there the system will invariably collapse.

Presently I will not consider that within some societies interest conflicts are not based solely on economic considerations. For example, there may be religious, nationality, and other conflicts which have limited or no economic foundations, or are only linked in a very indirect way. Nor will I consider military campaigns and wars, nor the special role of the military – which from the perspective of the ruling elite – always has a domestic as well as an external defense function. At the same time, since the military is a tool of expansionism, an aggressive society can with an imperialist policy increase the amount of goods that are available for distribution. Finally, there are societies that are exceptions to the overall rule, since a few have been able to provide for a strong military and an extensive system of surveillance and control without reducing the standards of living. However, this does not contradict the overall validity of the model that I have constructed. Exceptions to the rule or model, simply require that I examine each case on its own merits.

Having a model of this nature available for our analysis of Romania, will sensitize us to the major factors that determine its mode of operation. The key factors or components are the (1) gross national product, (2) the amount of this product returned to society in the form of consumer goods, and (3) the share of this product given to the control mechanisms of the state. This will require an examination of (a) the society's standard of living, (b) the extent and intensity of social conflict and (c) the extent and

Introduction 3

prospects of social and political stability. In other words, how does the distribution or re-distribution of goods in society stabilize or destabilize the system.

Romania under Ceausescu can be understood by looking at the linkage and balance among the above factors. The linkage between gross national product, the share of the control mechanism, the standard of living in society, and the tensions generated by these will define the relative stability or instability of the system. Overall two polar models may be outlined. At one end of the spectrum we can distinguish a model wherein you have a maximum distribution of goods among the producers/consumers of society, with a minimum of these being reserved for the military and police forces of society. In this model the external policies are characterized by negotiated settlements and cooperative arrangements, while peace is assured via security alliances rather than military preparedness. Examples of this model might be Denmark, Costa Rica, Luxembourg or Liechtenstein. The other polar model is the obverse of the above. It is based on a distribution system that provides the smallest possible share of the goods for the consumers and producers. Instead it uses the goods produced by society to reward the guardians of society's stability. Thus, it maintains an immense, top-heavy and ever-present control system, which has a well developed apparatus for exercising repression. An excellent example of this model is Romania.

Czesław Miłosz maintained in his work *The Acquisition of Power* that "2% live well, the question is simply, how can we become part of that 2 percent." A comparison of the members of the *nomenklatura** system, the privileged elements, in terms of their numbers and overall percentages within the populations of the individual communist societies, provides material for interesting comparisons of similarities and differences between these systems. Miłosz's two percent estimate is probably a conservative measurement of the Polish case. Whatever may be the number of the privileged elite in Poland, there is no doubt that the ruling caste in

---

* *Nomenklatura* refers to one of the mechanism of Party control. It involved the classification of all significant positions of decision-making in the govrnmental and administrative hierarchy which can be filled only by the most reliable party cadres. In other words, it entails a dual record keeping function: on the one hand, keeping track of all positions that control "the commanding heights of power", and on the other hand, maintaining a list of potential eligible party activists to fill these positions. Combined with the principle of "democratic centralism" this has meant that control of leadership selection always remained firmly in the hands of the Party's top leaders.

Romania – considering both its numerical size and interests – is no longer simply a ruling elite, it is now a ruling class. Who belong to this ruling class?

As everywhere in Eastern Europe, this class is composed of the party oligarchy, the governmental administration and the coercive forces of state power. These are the elements that are the direct beneficiaries of political and economic privileges. Others who benefit less directly are the profiteers of the back market. The market of scarcity is dependent on the current leadership and the black marketeers are dependent on the market of scarcity. Romania differs from Poland not so much in the make-up of its privileged sector but in its mass. That is, in Romania we are faced with a much larger coopted share of the population.

In relation to the Romanian armed forces, we have relatively dependable evaluations from Western military analysts.* Their estimates do not significantly alter the overall picture presented in official sources. The size of the armed forces is roughly analogous – in proportion to Romania's population – with the armed forces of other East European states.

Of Romania's 23,836,000 inhabitants, a little more than two-fifths is considered to be part of the active work force, or about 11.5 million people. On the basis of the available data Romania's armed forces on land, air and sea are under the leadership of professional commissioned and uncommissioned officers numbering 110,000. This is about 1 percent of the active workforce.

The number of those who have been drafted constitutes 70,000 at any given moment. To this number we also have to add the 20,000 security units of the Ministry of Defense which have to deal with demonstrations, strikes, or other anti-state activities.

These units are specifically trained to crush manifestations of opposition. Still another 20,000 constitute Romania's border guard. This means that an additional 1 percent of Romania's workforce is engaged for "security" purposes. While it is true that the draftees are sometimes utilized at construction sites or at harvest time, it is also true that this does not make up for their missed labor in the regular workforce.

The distortions only begin here. What follows is what makes Romania such an exception in the overall European context, this being the mobilized

---

* See particularly the annual yearbooks of NATO. For the present discussion I have drawn on the data presented in the report: "The Military Balance 1988-89" in the compilation provided by the London-based International Institute for Strategic Studies.

militarization of society at large. Civil defense organizations criss-cross society in a tightly woven network, penetrating every school, university and place of employment. In addition to this (and this is exceptional even for the region) even university co-eds are required to attend theoretical and practical training sessions in military science. Every institution of higher education has this requirement one month every year, and one day every week. The co-eds are trained by professional women officers who are encouraged to pursue this career by attractive financial considerations.

Paramilitary organization – a kind of patriotic guard or citizens' guard – also exists and includes about one-quarter million members. According to Western estimates, of the above, the active full-time professionals responsible for training the rank and file, constitute about 12,000. On the basis of my personal observations, this estimate is probably too low. This kind of paramilitary activity is easier to hide or disguise than the regular armed forces. But even if we accept the 250,000 estimate, it is clear that militarization of society is extensive and contributes to the economic problems of Romania.

At this point we cannot avoid mentioning a related problem. With the militarization of society there is a confusion of roles concerning the Romanian armed forces. The Romanian military is not viewed first and foremost as the defender of the country's security against external aggression. Instead, as in all dictatorships, the military's role is viewed as a brake on society to perpetuate the ruling minority's political monopoly. This is evident in the frequent mixed patrols (joint military and police patrols) that are evident on the city streets of Romanian cities, and which are also stationed at the more important production centers of the country (mines, energy generation plants, etc.). Furthermore, on occasion some of these enterprises even have military administrations. In this way, the internal control function of the Romanian armed forces and paramilitary organizations is much more important than what one could assume on the basis of just the raw data concerning the numbers of people affiliated with the military network.

Still it is already evident from the above that Romanian society must provide for the needs of a relatively larger proportion of its people who are engaged as part of the professional military, or whose capabilities, energy and time is devoted to security concerns. Yet in itself, this would still not constitute an impossible burden.

Romania's secret police – the notorious *Securitate* – its security and intelligence gathering organization is the most bloated in all of Eastern

Europe. Testimony based on empirical evidence is available on this in the writings of Romanian security operatives who defected to the West.* The insecurity of the present Romanian political establishment has brought into being an apparatus of control, that overshadows in both its methods and numerical size its counterparts in neighboring states. This fearsome control system is organized to monitor any and all processes or developments within society and to crush any opposition to the leadership. At the same time, it attempts to neutralize or eliminate opposition or resistance through preventive measures.

There is no official information about the size of the law enforcement agency called the "Militia." Attila Ara-Kovács, of the Transylvanian Hungarian Information Agency in Budapest, estimates that their number is about a quarter-million. This takes into account the fact that Romania has about 14,000 community settlements, and that even the smallest has its own Militiaman (who resides in a neighboring village or the county seat), while in the cities their numbers are very high (purposely high, to have an intimidating effect). If we also add to their numbers those of the traffic police and the economic enterprise guards, then the estimates of Attila Ara-Kovács are acceptable, although probably conservative. At any rate, this adds up to another 2.2 percent of the workforce.

If we try to estimate all the individuals who are employed in some way by the Ministry of Interior and its secret police and assume that each settlement must have at least one operative, then the minimum number is automatically 14,000. If we then add to this the Ministry of Interior's city organizations located in the county centers, where they usually occupy fortress-like buildings occupying half a city block, and their operatives who infiltrate all enterprises, educational institutions, labor unions, churches, clubs and other organizations, then – even if we only count 2,500 personnel per county, including everyone from the detective to the commanding general, the passport office employees and the workplace informers, and the bodyguards of the Presidential family and all the special security units of the state, then it is highly unlikely that the size of the security police is less than 100,000. In other words, we are again talking about an additional 1 percent of the workforce.

In summarizing the number of people who are part of the coercive establishments, we have 2 percent who are in active military service. The

---

* Ion Mihai Pacepa's *Red Horizons* (see endnote 38) provides the most extensive revelations about the operations of Romania's surveillance, security and intelligence network.

paramilitary services and the intelligence services are estimated to engage 0.5 percent (55-60,000), the police constitute 2.2 percent, and the secret police 1 percent. This means that a total of 6% of the active workforce is employed by some coercive agency. Subtracting from this the number of draftees, we still have 5 percent who compose the hard core of the political establishment's armed protectors. This hard core is willing to defend its own interests and the interests and privileges of allies, with both tooth and nail.

Who are the allies of this defensive hard core? First of all, the political elite, the members of the *nomenklatura* system, and the top levels of the State's governmental administration. Proportionate to its population, Romania has the most communists in the world: 3.64 million party members. (This is a December, 1986 statistic, by the end of 1989, it was 4 million.) In comparing Romania with its 23.8 million inhabitants to Hungary with its 10.6 million inhabitants, we find that at the beginning of 1989, Hungary had 0.8 million party members just before the drastic decline began. In other words, in Romania every fifth person is a party member, while in Hungary less than one in eleven is a party member.

Membership in the Young Communist organizations parallels the above party membership profile. According to available data, by 1989, they had also passed the 4 million mark. In this instance a chronological comparison with the USSR is very telling. In 1955, in the Soviet Union, 3.6 percent were communist while only 3.4 percent were communist in Romania. Seven years later, in 1962, of the Soviet population, 4.5 percent were communists while in Romania 4.9 percent were communists. Then Ceausescu came to power in 1965. Just eleven years later, 6.1 percent in the Soviet Union and 12 percent in Romania were communists. Today in Romania the percentage has risen over 16 percent.*

The fact that Romania has two to three times as many communists and members of the Young Communist organization as other communist political systems, naturally means that Romanian society must provide for the upkeep of two to three times as many party secretaries, party activists, regional, city and county party committee members and organizers. Because the party is everywhere, in the regional context and in each and every settlement, here too we must count at least 100,000 activists. Its presence everywhere also makes the party unchallengeable and infallible

---

* For the data at the end of the 1970's, see Paul S. Shoup (ed.), *The East European and Soviet Data Handbook* (New York, 1981).

in the direction of economic life, social organization, lawmaking, law enforcement, control of cultural expression and the role of the media.

Linked to all of the above, we still have to consider the governmental bureaucracy, the guiding force in the economic-social-cultural realm. While it is totally subservient to party direction, it is likewise top-heavy and inseparably intertwined with it in personnel and its vested interest in the *status quo*. From the village, city and county peoples' councils to the administrators of state enterprises, from numerous and overly bureaucratized ministries to the functionaries of the Democratic Socialist Unity Front, from the labor unions and women's organizations to the network of activists that control the communications media, the Romanian governmental set-up probably holds a world record as a sustainer of drones.

Those who belong to the privileged categories discussed so far, are all part of Romania's upper crust. In terms of their living standards, they are members of another country. It is out of these categories that Romania's "higher" echelon is composed. If they could also have free use of their passports, they could be considered privileged demigods. The unparalleled fusion of legislative, judicial and executive, policy-making and monitoring functions of government, merged with indistinguishable personal, family and special interest ties, provides Romania with a complex but homogeneous and self-conscious stratum composing 20-25% of the population. What binds them together is their vested interest in the existing distribution of goods, status and power. Family dependents of all those who compose the ruling caste, have been conservatively estimated as "two" for every "one" in the employed category. While the overall 20-25% is a minority, it is a large minority which controls all the instruments of power so that it can retain its monopoly of control and leadership.

Let us also cast a brief look at the outer circle of this privileged political establishment. Who do we find in this outer circle?

The outer circle includes all those who make a living by providing services for the establishment. Here I am thinking of such "responsible servant" positions as correspondence secretaries, letter openers, technicians charged with installing bugging devices, drivers and chauffeurs, physicians, cooks, tailors, barbers and others who take care of the day-to-day needs of the leaders of the party, government and armed services. In other words, the people who are entrusted with the housekeeping chores of the powerful.

The next outer circle includes people who feel vulnerable, and consequently out of fear or opportunism tie their destiny to the maintenance of the *status quo*. They do this generally because of personal weakness, and for a minimal payoff, the illusory feeling that they have more security in case employment opportunities change. For this illusory security they are willing to become informers for the surveillance system and provide regular reports to the police about their co-workers, neighbors or their acquaintances. In Romania the law even demands this kind of tattling when people have contacts with foreigners. The number of these "informers" in Romania is mind-boggling. The previously quoted book by Ion Pacepa includes extensive data about this. According to his report, present-day Romania has the largest number of informers in the "Socialist camp."

These people may no longer even be tied to the system by the petty awards or privileges they may have gotten, much more important as a tie is their compromised conscience. They now fear that a political turnaround may actually lead to revelations, to the publication of their reports, which would destroy their credibility in society. In a real sense they have become hapless prisoners of the system. They cannot turn against the system because it has too much "dirt" on them.

A much smaller group within the "outer circle" are the black marketeers. However, because of the catastrophic condition of the economy, this group is actually influential and indispensable. While they benefit from the overall misery of the economic situation, they also pump life into an otherwise unworkable system. In this way the "second economy" may make a difference for both the power structure and the man in the street. For the latter the "black market" can also make the difference between life and death, if it is only through this network that a person can obtain needed medication or gasoline. Gasoline can also be a life-saver if, for example, the individual has already used up his monthly quota of 25 liters, and needs to make an emergency run to the hospital, because the ambulances of the latter are grounded for lack of fuel! At any rate the black marketeer network includes an ever expanding number of smugglers, money launderers, sellers and re-sellers of smuggled or stolen goods. Those who are engaged in this kind of illicit enterprise, make excessive profits. Because of this, they have a sunk cost in the preservation of this system. Their numbers overall may not be large but they are strategically located and support the *status quo* that works to their personal financial benefit.

From the perspective of our overall concern, the role of women deserves attention. While in Poland 95 percent of the workforce provides for the needs of the remaining 5 percent, of the 95 percent the burden shared by women is not quite half, or 45 percent. In Romania, on the other hand, where 75 percent have to provide for the needs of 25 percent, the consequence for Romania's women population is an increased burden. Of the 75 percent almost half, or about 35 percent are women. However, even if they provide a smaller proportion of the active workforce than their Polish counterparts, they have to carry the weight of more drones. In other words, if we consider the overall sharing of work responsibilities, we find that in Romania seven women have proportionately the same amount of burden as nine women would have in Poland. This comes on top of more adverse conditions in Romania in relation to such things as the provision of basic foodstuffs, and intense social stresses that target women in particular. For example, in Romania abortion is strictly forbidden, it is a "criminal offense." At the same time, civilized birth control devices such as condoms, diaphragms, etc. are also forbidden and unavailable, except at great expense on the black market. Also on top of this is the male-dominant worldview of Romanian society. Relegated to such a subservient position women are not likely to become the catalyst for a resistance movement. One example will suffice to contradict the official lip-service paid to the equality of sexes. Although it is the women who bear children even in Romania, governmental "child-support" payments, as nominal as they are, are always paid to "the head of the family" (the menfolk) and not the mothers.

This essay has sought an answer to the question: why is there no effective opposition in any part of Romanian society that might challenge the oppression of the political establishment? There must be some oppressed minority that has nothing to lose and is therefore willing to become the center of resistance to the power structure. Furthermore, the power-structure must have some weak spot, some vulnerable point where pressure would lead to its collapse. After all, the power is monopolized by a minority, even if it is a significant minority of 20-25 percent of the population. In opposition to this ruling caste, with its unwilling allies, stands two-thirds or three-fourths of the population. And this vast number -in spite of the downtrodden condition of women in Romania – would seem a large enough majority to sweep away the tyrannical minority if the conditions were right. Because the majority must be able to recognize that its enemy and oppressor is this tyrant minority.

If this is how things are, if two-thirds or three-fourths of Romanian society is exploited, oppressed and humiliated, then one would think that the numerical superiority of the underdog, the lowest of the low, would be enough to produce a movement which would destroy this degenerate, distorted, and anti-social power-structure. It would be enough if it were united, but united it is not.

First of all, it is disunited ethnically. While the ruling "upper crust" of Romania is 99.99 percent composed of "pure" ethnic Romanians, the remaining three-fourths include a disproportionately larger representation of other ethnic groups. (In a population of 100 people, 10 Eskimos constitute 10% of the population, but if out of this 100 a separate ruling caste of 25 is established without Eskimos, then within the subordinate 75 the 10 Eskimos will now constitute not 10% but 15%.) This is parallel to what exists in Romania, and is a partial explanation for why the ethnic/nationality minorities are not in the forefront to dismantle the power-structure by force.

In this way the ethnic profile of Romania as a whole is not the same profile as the profile of the "ruling upper crust" or the profile of the remaining 75 percent. Even the 75 percent can be subdivided into the "lower part" and the "lowest part". The Gypsies, for example, are all situated in the "lowest part" from a socio-economic perspective. Those of them who are Hungarian in speech are always designated as "Gypsies" in the census, while those that speak the Gypsy language become Romanians according to the census. The Gypsy population of Romania is all in the "lowest part," all 1.4-1.6 million of them. The census does not admit this many. However, Romanian census results have been notorious for their "ethnic" manipulation. Between the two World Wars, the official census claimed that only 250,000 Gypsies lived in Romania. Fifty years later, according to the 1977 census, only 230,000 Gypsies were counted. This is an absurdity as well as an outright lie. The Gypsies are probably the only ethnic group that still retain their commitment to large families and many children! However, whatever their actual numbers in the population, since they have not developed their own middle class, they lack the stratum that could provide them with leadership in a resistance movement. In this sense, at the present time, the Gypsies have to be discounted as part of the 75 percent that is willing to rebell against the power structure.

Unfortunately, the same applies to the other ethnic/national minorities. The Jews -who survived World War II – have been all but eliminated by the mass migration to Israel. The German minorities are also in the last stages of their evacuation from Transylvania. Even the Hungarians – or at least their intellectuals – are becoming more and more familiar with the option of emigration. All three of the latter, as well as the remaining Slavic and Turkish minorities now focus their attention on bettering their conditions by emigrating rather than by trying to reform the system that grinds them into the ground. For most of them this option is relatively painless, because they have a "motherland" in close proximity geographically. For the Jews this is also understandable because of the legacy of intolerance that has surrounded them in Romania. Barely had they come out of the shock of the Holocaust and the Romanian pogroms of the 1940s when at the end of the 1950s, they had to face a revived anti-Semitism. Emigration seemed the only logical escape-hatch. For the Hungarians and Germans the intolerance was framed as their "collective war guilt." They were the objects of constant intimidation, with the threat of expulsion and extermination constantly hanging over their heads. This was brought home to them in forced labor settlements, pogroms, extermination camps, and expulsions. The constant repetition of "war guilt" made the two largest minorities cautious and passive. The decision of the minorities to choose emigration, almost instinctively, rather than resistance, is decimating the best elements and the most self-conscious sectors of the skilled working class and the intellectuals. This is a major loss not just for the minorities but for Romania also, because minorities always constituted an important part of its middle class and the elite of its skilled workers. But perhaps this is the intent of the Romanian power-structure: the decapitation of the potential opposition. It is pretty evident to most observers that without intellectuals and a self-conscious working class, it is very difficult to establish a core of resistance. With the emigration of Jewish, German, and Hungarian intellectuals, Romania is sinking into a kind of helpless Eastern torpor, out of which – at least from within – it will be very difficult to shake free.

The key role of the minorities is closely linked to the relative weakness of the ethnic Romanian intelligentsia. Unlike the Polish, Czechoslovak or Hungarian middle class, the Romanian middle class suffered much more devastation from the effects of communist rule. Because of the unique distortions of the Romanian system, the re-emergence of an independent intellectual sector of society is much less likely. In part this is due to the inability of the – numerically small – middle class elite to break with the kind of nationalism that Ceausescu uses as his instrument to persecute the national minorities and to undermine the prospects for democracy.

Another reason why developments have taken the direction they have is that Romanian society lacks the kind of political traditions which sanctify radical opposition to authoritarian government. The fact is that Romanian energies – or at least most of them – have not been guided by the desire to become a part of Europe intellectually or spiritually. Since 1919, with the creation of Greater Romania the nation as a whole, including most of its intellectuals as well, has been absorbed in a kind of digestive obsession. Romanian society has seen as its primary task the absorbtion and assimilation of the cultures and peoples that were incorporated with the engorged territory. This obsession has led to a neglect of democratic and constitutional reforms.

It is in this light that many people have accused the emigrating minority intellectuals of betraying not only their own people – for example the Hungarians of Transylvania – but also Romanian society at large. Parallel to this, the Romanian intellectuals are also responsible for neglect of duty. They have bought into the mass psychosis that the minorities must be digested and eliminated. Thus Romania's historic opportunity to provide a program of ethical and spiritual guidance has been betrayed by the short-sighted quest of establishing a homogeneous nation-state. The intellectuals failed to recognize that by eliminating minorities – practicing ethnocide – they were setting the stage for their own enslavement. For some reason they did not see – or did not want to see – that the elimination of schools teaching in the languages of the national minorities, would ultimately lead to the elimination of their own schools. That intolerance for instruction in a different language can easily become translated into intolerance of what is taught in any language. Hating what is different in languages can then also lead to hating what is envisioned by others. In this kind of environment there can be only one official language and only one acceptable system of ideas.

To summarize the foregoing: Romania has become an autocratic social-economic-political system, in which roughly one-fourth of the population has a vested interest. This one-fourth is the most homogeneous and unified sector of society ethnically and in terms of interests. It monopolizes political and coercive control over society. The remaining three-fourths of Romanian society is not unified or homogeneous. Although it is exploited by the "ruling upper crust," it has not been able to take a united stand in favor of a radical transformation of the political order. Differences in ethnic, cultural origins, traditions and interests, have kept them from being able to define common goals and to take a united stand against the power-structure. This inability of the lower three-fourths to act as one is the tragedy of contemporary Romania.

This does not mean that the dictatorship governing Romania is a permanent fixture. However, we can assume that an internal collapse of the system is not likely. The present socio-economic and political profile of Romania does not seem to possess the kind of reserves or hidden potentials for resistance, the cumulative effect of which could lead to a successful challenge of the present power-structure.

At the same time, in 1987, the workers' rebellion in Braşov (Brassó) – in reality a desperate Jacquerie sparked by hunger and famine conditions – and the public criticism of Ceausescu by six important party veterans and some poets in the spring of 1989, led some observers to talk about the coming collapse of this system. However, due to the atomized nature of Romanian society, these events and other acts of resistance could be isolated, and therefore they did not become a chain of events that could activate a coherent opposition movement. In large part the present essay was written in 1987 to warn people not to expect the imminent collapse of the regime, and that perhaps things will continue as always!

In other words, the power structure of Romania is such that it is capable of reproducing itself as long as it has its primary force of cohesion, the dictatorship and the dictator. Within the existing structure the will of this dictator is unquestionable and final. In this context the collapse of the structure is conceivable only if one of two scenarios occurs. One would be a major international or external challenge to the system. We cannot deal with such a prospect given the limitation of this essay. Secondly, if the dictator would die or significantly become impaired physically or mentally, this would lead to an internal struggle for succession. This in turn could lead to the kind of break-down or anarchy which might result in an overall collapse. Presently I will not deal with this scenario either, that is, the unlikely disappearance of the Ceausescu clan from the political scene. In the final analysis, Romania's internal power-structure will accommodate or acclimate to the external pressures that circumscribe the role of the country in the greater international environment. In turn, the survival of the power structure will depend on its ability to find acceptance and allies in that larger external context.

In conclusion, with the present analysis, I hope to have provided a better understanding of Romania for those who are unable, for example, to comprehend Ceausescu's village bulldozing plan. This was nothing more than the manifestation of Ceausescu's desire for total control, linked to his personality cult which was driven by the need to impose total conformity on society by eliminating all vestiges of cultural uniqueness, rural "backwardness," or a toleration of pluralism. Thus, this book helps to answer the questions: Why does Romania tolerate this kind of abject slavery? Why does Romanian society tolerate this systematic subjugation that leads to its rape and humiliation on a daily basis?

Géza Szőcs
Geneva, May, 1989.

Chapter I

Preliminary Observations

Increasingly alarming news is reaching the Hungarian and international public. The totalitarian regime of Romania, grappling with an ever more serious internal crisis, continues to violate basic human rights and political freedoms. The national and ethnic minorities of that country live in particularly difficult circumstances. Not only are they deprived of basic rights which all citizens ought to enjoy, but they are also hard hit by policies of discrimination. They are the objects of forced assimilation pursued by an extremely nationalistic (and sometimes blatantly racist) state power. The government encourages anti-minority and xenophobic feelings. It follows a policy of "divide and rule" in an effort to hinder the development of understanding between ethnic Romanians and the minority populations. In this way it hopes to prolong its anachronistic rule.

What has been perpetrated in Romania – through increasingly overt methods since 1980 – is a kind of cultural genocide.* The primary target of this campaign has been the more than two-million strong Hungarian ethnic community, the majority of whom live in Transylvania. They have been deprived of the right to use their own language, to preserve their culture, and their historical traditions. Both as a people and as individuals they have been reduced to a status of second-class citizenship. They have

---

* Cultural Genocide or Ethnocide is the extirpation of an ethnic or national community by depriving it of its culture. It has been coined to describe the systematic effort to undermine the cultural identity and cohesion of minorities by majorities (e.g. Romanization, Russification, etc.). This differs from "genocide" in that the group is not physically exterminated (eliminated), only deprived of cultural allegiance through policies of forced acculturation/assimilation (e.g. monolingual educational, social, political, economic, and cultural policies) which are driven by an intolerance of diversity and the eternal quest for homogeneity. By obstructing or destroying the institutional mechanism for the transmission of symbols, values, language and knowledge, a people subjected to this process disappears, or becomes "de-nationalized," by becoming part of another culture or "national community." One national identity forcibly replaces the previous national identity.

been deprived of their fundamental human rights on both the individual and collective level. It stands to reason that sensitivity in Hungary concerning the Hungarian minority living in Romania is intense. After all, those who are living on different sides of the state borders belong to one and the same nation, have common historical traditions and cultural values, and are linked together by the natural ties of family and friendship.

The authors of the present report cannot remain indifferent when Hungarians (or people of other nationalities) anywhere are discriminated against and when intellectual and material values of Hungarian (or any other) culture are threatened with destruction. This is why it is their duty to disseminate information and to raise an alarm. These tasks are indispensable especially in Central and Eastern Europe, where political borders do not coincide with ethnic boundaries and where the oppression of minorities has so often led to tragic conflicts. It is particularly dangerous within the context of Hungarian-Romanian relations. The tensions which the anti-Hungarian policies of today's Romanian regime is generating inside the country and in bilateral relations can result only in incalculable harm to the interests of both peoples. Coupled with other political and ethnic problems these tensions can become a permanent source of conflict with negative consequences for the entire European continent. Any effort to prevent the further deterioration of the situation is thus not only in the interest of the Hungarian minority, but is a matter of grave international concern. It is not limited merely to the bilateral relations between Hungarians and Romanians.

The present report intends to convey objective information to the international public about the situation of the Hungarian minority in Romania. Its compilers have been guided by a commitment to democratic rights, to equality among peoples and cultures, and to the self-determination of nations and national minorities. In this sense, the question of minorities is a question for all of mankind. Any solution of the problem worthy of the late twentieth century would require, above all, the easing of border barriers – in both the physical and spiritual sense of the term. The elimination of political borders as constraints, must be followed by a full guarantee of fundamental freedoms to the individuals and communities concerned. Particularly unacceptable is the arbitrary power of states to determine the language, culture, and ethnic identity of citizens living in areas which were acquired through territorial expansion, or partial or complete state succession.

The authors feel that the resolution of the nationality conflicts is ultimately dependent on historical processes and major social developments. These processes and developments will provide the momentum for eroding state borders in multi-national regions. This will allow the principles of self-determination, equality and sovereignty of nations to acquire new meaning. The prospects for a satisfactory resolution of this question is closely linked to the strengthening of democracy in a number of Central and East European states. The growth of democratic aspirations also fuels the quest for nationality emancipation.

The aim of the authors – researchers and publicists of Transylvanian and Hungarian origin representing different disciplines – has been to compile a short study based on recent data describing the present reality. The object of this report is not to present a historical survey or a comprehensive monograph covering the fate of the Hungarians in Romania. Works written along such lines in both Hungarian and other languages have already been published, and others are in the process of preparation. The present study, in addition to presenting the basic facts concerning the Hungarian minority, is primarily a summation of recent developments related to the subject.

The scarcity of reliable sources has made it extremely difficult to prepare an accurate and dependable situation report. There is hardly any official statistical data available on the Hungarian population of Romania. The figures that do exist tend to be either distorted or deliberately lifted out of context, thus severely limiting possibilities for longitudinal and other comparative studies. With very few exceptions, general fact-finding, empirical sociological studies – and not just those concerning minorities – are no longer undertaken in Romania. In the past the press published some data on minority schools, cultural institutions, and publishing activities but in recent years such information has been accorded the status of being "classified information." Under such circumstances, in addition to making use of Hungarian analyses, we must, therefore, rely upon estimates and communiqués issued by European scientific reviews and the mass media. Furthermore, we must utilize the communications and works of minority members themselves, who, understandably are reluctant to be exposed as the sources of such information.

For the above reasons, we cannot always provide the kind of precise data which the reader accustomed to international usage would otherwise justifiably expect. At other times we must refrain from referring to specific available documents and sources in order to protect the suppliers of the data. Thus, we have prepared a report on an ethnic community which is restricted in the knowledge of its true past, is denied an awareness of its present, and has no prospects in the future. At least the Romanian myth of "homogenization" would like them to acquiesce to this "status."

The authors completed the final version of this report following an extensive discussion devoted to it by the Hungarian Democratic Forum in March 1988 in Budapest. The final draft of the report took into consideration the various comments and suggestions submitted by the participants of these discussions.

Chapter II

Historical Considerations

It is virtually impossible to summarize in a few sentences, or to clarify in a few lines, Hungarian-Romanian relations concerning Transylvania. It is impossible to present such an overview because Hungarian-Romanian relations constitute a comprehensive, multifaceted, and historically determined system. Within this system one should distinguish, for example, between the relationships of the two states, the political parties, and the relations of two nations, Hungarian and Romanian. This must be done even if we cannot overcome the prejudices of the past. No matter what historical, economic, social, or ideological problems are involved in the coexistence of the two nations, it is certain that over the centuries Transylvania has been at the center of these relations. There can be no doubt that the Transylvanian question is of concern not only to Hungarians and Romanians but is also part of general European concerns, i.e., it influences relationships in a much wider region.

The dispute concerning Transylvania can be better understood if we have a clear view of its history.[1] This explains the lively interest in any statement made on Transylvania by historians of the two countries. For this reason the three-volume work entitled *Erdély története*[2], published recently in Budapest, became an immediate sensation. However, judging from the debate surrounding these volumes, and their official Romanian reception, it is apparent that historical arguments can never be absolute. They can be perverted, without regard for their accuracy in defining reality, so as to satisfy the demands of political exigencies. Concealment of historical facts or their manipulation for selfish ends by any nation demonstrates an abuse of history. Such practice discloses an inclination to appropriate historical arguments (e.g., ethnogenesis, or the matter of who ruled over a territory and when) to rationalize or justify a political goal of the present. This kind of history can lead only to charges and counter-charges.

With the above considerations in mind, we would like to present, by way of setting the scene, a few historical data pertaining to the subject matter. We do this, fully cognizant that the facts of history should be analyzed by professional historians. However, it is not by recourse to history alone that the case of Transylvania – and of the Hungarians who inhabit it – can be most accurately understood, particularly at the present time.

In the majority of European states, political borders have not coincided with ethnic boundaries either in the past or at present. The divergences between the two kinds of boundaries give rise to the existence of national, linguistic, ethnic, and other minorities. In the eastern half of Europe, this trend is even more pronounced. Ethnic groups have settlements over wide areas living in communities spilling over national boundaries, with different levels of national consciousness. Even the stages of national development often display substantial differences in their socio-economic foundations among different peoples.

In this region the division between "state nation" and "cultural nation" has produced intense antagonism. This leads to tensions within countries and can even lead to conflicts between nations and states. The number and intensity of these conflicts was increased by the territorial restructuring dictated by great-power interests after the First and Second World Wars. The restructuring failed to take into account the right of some nations to self-determination. For the Hungarians in particular, the problem of state-nation versus cultural-nation gained new significance because the Austro-Hungarian Monarchy collapsed and the territorial changes which followed World War I caused Hungary to lose not only territory but also one-third of its Hungarian ethnic population. Consequently, for the past seventy years one disturbing and destabilizing political-ethnographic fact of Europe is that one-third of the Hungarian nation lives in minority status beyond the present borders of Hungary. These Hungarian minorities are located for the most part in neighboring countries.

Romania acquired the largest territorial gains from historical Hungary in the redrawing of boundaries following the World War I. This included historical Transylvania (Erdély/Ardeal), the Bánság (Banat) region, and the Partium (Crisana) region.[2] These regions taken together constitute what we shall henceforth refer to as Transylvania* in today's broader and more widely accepted sense of the term. The territory ceded to Romania after 1920 had been part of the Kingdom of Hungary. In the 16th and 17th centuries, following the Turkish conquest which brought about the temporary disintegration of the Hungarian state, Transylvania existed for a time as an independent principality. It was in a loose dependency relationship with the Ottoman Empire, but continued to recognize the unity of the countries of the Hungarian Holy Crown. After liberation from Turkish domination, the principality of Transylvania associated itself with the Kingdom of Hungary. The 1848/49 Hungarian War of Independence, which transformed Hungary into a modern national state, also proclaimed the union of Hungary and Transylvania. However, actual unification came only after 1867 and continued to prevail until the end of World War I.

Transylvania has been the common homeland of several peoples – Hungarians, Romanians, Saxon-Germans and other nationalities – for nearly a thousand years. Its lot has been closely intertwined with the Hungarian, Romanian and German past, while its specific independent historical route has left deep impressions on the cultures and national consciousness of all of them. The relationships of these peoples have been influenced not only by the experiences of interdependence and interaction but also by conflicts and antagonisms of varying intensity.

From the point of view of reconciliation or the normalization of Hungarian-Romanian relations in Transylvania, in our opinion, it makes no difference whether the Hungarians are descendants of Sumerians or Scythians and whether, on the other side, the first known ancestors of Romanians were members of the Thracian-Getan-Dacian tribes or the soldiers of the Roman legions of Trajan. It is also futile and unnecessary to dwell upon whose forefathers were the first to set foot on the soil of Transylvania.

---

* Transylvania refers to the territories acquired by Romania from Hungary following World War I. However, not all of these territories were considered a part of historic Transylvania. It is none the less accurate to say that all regions acquired by Romania north of the Transylvanian Alps and west of the eastern Carpathian mountain ranges, including the lowlands of the Banat and Szatmár regions (the old Partium) have since that time been called Transylvania. This Latin designation means "land beyond the forest." The Hungarian name for the region is "Erdély" (forest covered land), which was then also adopted by the Romanians with a slightly different pronunciation and written as "Ardeal." The Saxon German designation for the historic Transylvania was Siebenbürgen (or the land of seven castles).

What is much more important is to examine the conditions of the inhabitants of Transylvania at the time of national awakening, which set in as a result of the Enlightenment, then of Romanticism, and economically speaking, the beginning of capitalist development, when they attained a sense of modern nationhood.

Hungarian historians believe that this period began in the last third of the 18th century, and found the Hungarians in a relatively advantageous position in Transylvania. This was the case in spite of the immense human and cultural losses suffered by ethnic Hungarians during Turkish domination and, of course, earlier as well. Even when they were at such a relative disadvantage in comparison to peoples of more fortunate regions of Europe, they played an important role in Transylvania. They managed to preserve vestiges of their statehood and partial elements of their institutional system, as well as their "state-forming" nobility which survived as well.

The elites of the non-Hungarian peoples of Hungary initially identified themselves with the Hungarian elite, spontaneously and without compulsion. Voluntary assimilation proceeded without a hitch as long as it relied on the prestige and authority of the medieval Kingdom of Hungary or was promoted later, in the 19th century, by the spontaneous forces of urbanization and industrialization.

A policy of forced assimilation in Hungary can be said to have been pursued only from the end of the 19th century. We do not wish to detract from the responsibility of earlier narrow-minded Hungarian governments for having nourished prejudice against the minorities at the turn of this century, but, at the same time, we should also emphasize another historical fact: the Austro-Hungarian Monarchy was a liberal state characterized by party pluralism, freedom of the press, a developed network of corporate and ecclesiastical, as well as cultural and economic institutions, which were also widely utilized by the minorities. This is why the legal status and effective position of the minorities at that time can in no way be compared to the situation of minorities living under emergent dictatorships and the totalitarian systems of the twentieth century.

The same historical tendencies prevailed in Transylvania as in other parts of the Hungarian kingdom. One significant difference as regards Hungarian and Romanian consciousness was that the institutions of the medieval Hungarian state – its feudal constitution, dating back to as early as 1437, from which the association of the "three nations" and the "four (established) denominations" was derived – remained virtually intact until

1848. The Romanians were not represented in these institutions, although they had grown to be the most numerous people of Transylvania by the middle of the 18th century. This situation was, of course, seriously detrimental to the Romanian intellectual movement which was unfolding in Transylvania at that time. On the other hand, all this also offered the Habsburg Monarchy a convenient opportunity for political manipulation in its effort to loosen the solidly Hungarian and Protestant character of the internal political-ideological and religious order of Transylvania. The Catholicization of some of the Romanians with the establishment of a religious union through the Greek Catholic (Uniate) Church, and the promised possibility that converts would enjoy the same privileges as the priests and adherents of the Roman Catholic Church, provided Vienna with an effective political weapon, that it could employ at will. Simultaneously, attending Catholic schools provided the Romanians of Transylvania with the golden opportunity for advancement through their own church structure. This enabled their intellegentsia, of clerical and gentry origin, to forge a separate national consciousness. Instead of assimilating into the Hungarian county nobility and, in so doing, losing touch with the Romanian population as had been the case in earlier centuries, they became a self-conscious leadership stratum for the Romanians.

The position of the Romanians had been very unfavorable. Their aim, to be admitted into the social-political order of the Transylvanian feudal constitution, could be achieved only by enlarging or breaking through the established feudal framework. Consequently, the set of arguments which they developed (the doctrine of Daco-Romanian autochthonism) to justify their demands, was itself a grievance-generated conception, based on a feudal perception of rights. The Romanians accounted for their disadvantaged status solely and exclusively to their conquest and political subjection. In this perception no consideration is given to the complete absence of a nobility of their own, equal in status to the Hungarian nobility. Also neglected is the dynamics of a natural process of assimilation and integration of the Romanian nobility by the Hungarian nobility, driven by considerations of power and prestige.

As soon as this theory emerged it provided Romanians emotional commitments and attitudes that justified their oppositional posture to the *status quo*. This undermined any chance to objectively examine the extent to which the theory tallied with reality. All this, of course, also meant that this new national self-definition acquired simultaneously a dogmatic ideological character which has prevailed up through the present.

Rather than enumerating historical arguments and counter-arguments, it would be more beneficial to inquire into a possible way out of the present situation in which Hungarian-Romanian relations have become dangerously mired. Even at the level of personal contacts, relations have been poisoned to the extent that current social, political, and economic relations reflect it in Central and Eastern Europe. The best sons and daughters of both peoples need to be made aware that many more historical circumstances argue for their peaceful coexistence than for their relentless animosity. And last, but not least, their present condition is not preordained and irreversible. Examples of possible reconciliation can be found in the recent past of Western Europe, e.g., the normalization of Franco-German relations. For this to take place, however, every Hungarian and Romanian possessing a sense of responsibility must understand that this is not feasible without mutual and concerted efforts and particularly not without a lot of patience and mutual toleration.

Much, therefore, remains yet to be done. However, the "bridge" of friendly relations linking the peoples of the two countries must be constructed at long last. The pillars of this bridge must be built upon a solid and strong foundation of Romanian and Hungarian identity rooted in universal human values, both in Hungary and in Romania.

Chapter III

The Population Profile of the Hungarians in Romania

The 1980 census in Hungary puts the total population of the country at 10,710,000 inhabitants. According to various statistics, surveys and estimates, some 250-500 thousand are of non-Hungarian origin, i.e., belong to national and ethnic minorities. The latest censuses conducted in the neighboring states showed the number of inhabitants of Hungarian nationality or Hungarian speaking to be as follows:[3] Czechoslovakia – 630,000 (700,000); Soviet Union – 171,000 (200,000); Romania – 1,670,000 (2.1 to 2.2 million); Yugoslavia – 420,000 (460,000); and, Austria – 50,000. The latter figure includes the original Hungarian settlements of Burgenland, as well as Hungarian groups dispersed throughout Austria. According to estimates based on various criteria, the Hungarian diaspora in the West, mainly in North America and Western Europe, numbers between 1.0 and 1.5 million. Few other ethnic communities within and outside Europe are characterized by a similar geographical dispersion and political fragmentation.[4] Owing to this fact, the minority question constitutes a fundamental social, cultural, and political issue for Hungary and for the Hungarian nation as a whole.

The Hungarians of Romania, by virtue of their numbers and cultural development, are the most significant Hungarian ethnic group outside Hungary. They are the largest national minority in Europe, and this fact in itself lends considerable political weight to any change in their status.

The Hungarian inhabitants of Romania are citizens of a multinational state comprised of regional units. These units have undergone different historical and cultural developments, and have evolved different ways of life. From the perspective of its social and cultural features, Transylvania is the most developed and diversified region in the country and the most heterogeneous in terms of its ethnic composition. Historical differences manifest themselves not only, and not even primarily, in statistical indices but more in the form of competing and conflicting cultures, value systems, and lifestyles adopted by particular regions and communities.[5] In an attempt to obliterate historical and cultural diversity, official Romanian policy attempts to establish a "unified Romanian national state." This is linked to the policy of "homogenization" and the general lowering of the socio-economic status of the entire population, particularly to the detriment of both the minorities and the Romanians living in Transylvania.

The last census in Romania (1977) recorded a total population of 21,559,910 inhabitants, of which 10.9% (2,352,419) belonged to national minorities.[6] A breakdown of the country's population with respect to national and linguistic affiliation, based on the official census data for the period 1948 to 1977, is presented in Table 1.

According to the Hungarian census conducted in 1910, there were 1,670,000 Hungarian-speaking people in the territory ceded to Romania after World War I. Following both World Wars, the Hungarian population suffered a considerable decline as a consequence of population transfers. Transfers continued in smaller numbers after 1945, then picked up again after 1980. According to official statistics, the number of Hungarians increased by 10% between 1948-56, but then came to a sudden halt. In actuality, the rate of natural increase among Hungarians remained relatively high, although the actual increase in numbers was not reflected in either the 1966 or 1977 censuses.[7] Neither assimilation into the ethnic Romanian population nor emigration is able to account for the above discrepancies and is most likely the result of misrepresentations in the counting of the population.

The census of 1956 was the last census to publish data on nationalities by settlements (villages, etc.). We are therefore compelled to rely upon its data alone for representing the territorial distribution of Hungarians. Consequently, our data reflects the situation of more than thirty years ago. Since that time the overall percentage of minorities living in cities has been reduced. No general census has been conducted in Romania since 1977. At a party conference in December 1987, the president of Romania merely announced that the population of the country had risen to 23 million. However, taking into consideration the natural demographic trends and ethnic distribution along religious lines in Transylvania, the present number of Hungarians in Romania must be, according to conservative estimates, between 2.1 and 2.2 million, i.e., 9.5% of the total population.[8]

Table 1
Distribution of the Romanian Population by Ethnic Group and Mother Tongue (censuses of 1948-1977)

Population	1948 by mother tongue	1956 by mother tongue	1956 by nationality	1966 by mother tongue	1966 by nationality	1977 by nationality*	1977 by nationality & mother tongue**
Number in thousands							
Romanian	13,598	15,081	14,996	16,771	16,747	19,004	19,207
Hungarian	1,500	1,654	1,588	1,652	1,620	1,707	1,671
German	344	395	383	388	383	359	332
Jewish (Yiddish)	139	134	146	5	43	26	25
Gypsy	-	67	104	49	64	230	76
Other	292	258	270	238	246	233	248 ***
Total	15,873	17,489	17,489	19,103	19,103	21,559	21,559
In percentages							
Romanian	85.7	86.2	85.7	87.8	87.7	88.1	89.1
Hungarian	9.4	9.5	9.1	8.6	8.5	7.9	7.8
German	2.2	2.2	2.2	2.0	2.0	1.7	1.5
Jewish (Yiddish)	0.9	0.2	0.8	x	0.2	0.1	0.1
Gypsy	-	0.4	0.6	0.3	0.3	1.1	0.4
Other	1.8	1.5	1.6	1.3	1.3	1.1	1.1
Total	100.0	100.0	100.0	100.0	100.0	100.0	100.0

*Based on preliminary census data.
**Based on definitive census data.
*** Of which: 44,875 were of "different tongues and nationalities."

Source: Romanian statistical data published in *Erdély története* [A History of Transylvania] (Budapest, 1986), Vol. 3, 1766.

The overwhelming majority of the people of Hungarian nationality lives on the territory annexed by Romania under the Treaty of Trianon, i.e., in Transylvania. Other major groups of Hungarians outside this region are in Bacău (Bákó) county in Moldavia and in Bucharest, the capital of Romania.

The earliest Hungarian settlers in Moldavia are known as "Csángó." This particular ethnic Hungarian community, separated long ago from the

Székelys* of Transylvania, has for centuries existed in Romanian surroundings outside the borders of the Hungarian state, east of the Carpathians. For historical and geographical reasons, this group of Hungarians is the most seriously endangered by Romania's policy of forced assimilation. They have been completely isolated from the outside world by the Romanian government. They have no Hungarian-language schools at present and were allowed virtually none in the past, with the exception of a very limited number in the period following World War II.[9]

The Hungarians of Moldavia have remained faithful to Catholicism in a Romanian Orthodox sea. From the Middle Ages to the present, their religion has preserved their distinct identity. At the same time, however, their priests were unfamiliar with the Hungarian language. This contributed to a decline in the use of their mother tongue. In the 1600s the Vatican sent monks and priests who spoke Hungarian poorly or not at all, to the Hungarian-inhabited settlements of Moldavia. Later from the latter half of the 19th century the creation of the Kingdom of Romania and the growth of nationalism changed the situation of the Csángós from bad to worse. Romanian became the official state language and also the language of sermons and prayers in the Hungarian churches. The forced assimilation of the Csángó Hungarians became a prelude to the anti-minority policies pursued by Romania following its expansion after the World War I. These policies have been implemented through a systematic campaign conducted with increasing ruthlessness to the present writing. Nearly all Moldavian Catholics are of Hungarian descent and their number far exceeds 100,000. Those whose mother tongue is still Hungarian, number about 70-80 thousand at the end of the 1980s.

The breakdown of the population by religious affiliation largely corresponds to the national groupings of Romania. The Hungarians are mostly Catholics and Calvinists, while others are Unitarians or belong to one of the smaller Protestant denominations. Table 2 presents the regional distribution of Hungarians, while Table 3 presents the distribution and numbers of their religious denominations.

The 1977 census showed 22% of the total population of Transylvania to be Hungarian. Other nationalities inhabiting this region in substantial numbers are Germans (Saxons and Swabians), South Slavs, Slovaks,

---

* The Székelys, or Szeklers as they are sometimes called, are a distinct ethnic subgroup within the Transylvanian Hungarian population. They possess distinct territorial settlements and distinct cultural traits.

Ukrainians, Jews, and Gypsies. According to the 1977 census, the ethnic minorities comprise 29.1% of the total population of the region. The estimated Hungarian ratio of the total population of Transylvania today exceeds 24%. A large concentration of Hungarians live in some 500 communities in the Székely region. The geographical expanse of this region coincides roughly with the administrative territory of the earlier Hungarian Autonomous Region. This Region had been formed in 1952 but was later dissolved in 1960 through an administrative reorganization of Romania. Despite the new administrative limits – detrimental to the Hungarian minority – and continuous Romanian mass immigration into the area, the proportion of Hungarians in the populations of the two counties of Harghita (Hargita) and Covasna (Kovászna) in the Székely region still exceeds 80% and 70% respectively, while in Mureş (Maros) county it is a little below 50%. Other important Hungarian-inhabited districts are located in the border zone with Hungary, mainly in Satu-Mare (Szatmár), Bihor (Bihar) and Arad and in the central counties of Cluj (Kolozs), and Sălaj (Szilágy) in the northwestern part of Romania.

Table 2
Estimates of the Number of Hungarians in Romania by Major Hungarian-Inhabited Areas (1977 and 1987)

Regional Area	1977 Census	1977 Estimate	1987 Estimate
Transylvania	1,651,000	1,850,000	2,030,000
Bacău county	4,000	80,000	70,000
Bucharest	8,000	100,000	100,000
Remaining parts of Romania	8,000	?	?
Total	1,671,000	2,030,000	2,200,000

Despite relatively dense settlement patterns, the Hungarian minority, under Romania's current system lacks any sort of economic and social autonomy. Subordination and overcentralization characterizes all aspects of life. The material bases of self-government and self-administration, along with pertinent political conditions, were completely abolished in the 1950s. Furthermore, by the end of the 1970s, the methods of "war communism" were introduced into economic management. Moreover, in recent years even the cultivation of household plots in villages has been subjected to central economic planning. In December 1981 an exceptionally severe "decree on labor discipline" was issued, and in January 1985 direct military administration was established in industrial concerns declared to be of "vital importance."

Table 3
The Number of Hungarians in Romania as Estimated on the Basis of Religious Affiliation (1987)

Religious Affiliation	Number of Parishoners
Roman Catholics	950,000
Roman Catholics of Hungarian mother tongue in the Iasi diocese (Csángók)	70,000
Roman Catholics of Hungarian mother tongue in the Bucharest diocese	30,000
Calvinists	800,000
Unitarians	80,000
Lutherans	30,000
Other Protestants	90,000
Former Greek Catholics unregistered in the records of parishoners	80,000
Total	2,130,000

Under such conditions, economic units (enterprises and production cooperatives) enjoy no freedom to pursue local objectives either in respect to development or profit utilization. They are strictly dependent upon the decision-making center, which is, in most cases, geographically remote. It controls contacts between economic units by issuing administrative ordinances. Thus, the central planning system, coupled with control over the locating of industrial projects, has proven to be a useful means of hindering closer cooperation and integration between Hungarian-inhabited regions. Control over transportation and communication on both the individual and communal level has reduced contacts among minority settlements to a minimum.

State-control over the location of industry has dispersed compact ethnic settlements. The central policy of "relocating" specialists, has also brought a substantial change in the ethnic composition of Transylvanian cities, notably those of Cluj (Kolozsvár), Timişoara (Temesvár), Oradea (Nagyvárad), Braşov, Tîrgu-Mureş (Marosvásárhely). An important result of the territorial and social fragmentation of the Hungarian population in Romania is that a large part of the Hungarian population is being scattered. While Hungarians, along with Germans and Jews, comprised the overwhelming bulk of the population in Transylvanian cities before 1945, now they have become minorities even in those urban centers.[10]

In Romania citizens are not guaranteed the right to freely choose their places of work and residence. Consequently the minority population is helpless in the face of governmental policies that seek to disrupt their unity and traditional settlement patterns. The origin of these policies date back to Romania's considerable territorial aggrandizement following World War I, although some elements of it were already visible in Romanian politics at the turn of the century.

Migration from Romanian-inhabited territories – mainly from the pre-1920 royal Romanian provinces of Moldavia and Wallachia – to Transylvanian towns and industrial centers began to increase in 1948, the year of the establishment of the totalitarian regime. However, the migration sharply accelerated after 1975. Romanian professionals who are willing to take up residence in districts inhabited mainly by Hungarians receive benefits and incentives. For example, they may apply for a so-called resettlement allowance of 15-30 thousand lei.* The immigration of other social strata is encouraged by additional economic measures. Parallel to this process, Hungarian intellectuals and professionals from Transylvania, upon completing their studies, are assigned to Romanian-inhabited districts, far from their place of birth. This strictly centralized system of work assignment provides the authorities far-reaching opportunities for manipulation. Consequently, fewer and fewer Hungarian teachers, physicians, agronomists, and other professionals can find jobs in Hungarian-inhabited areas.[11]

This practice undermines the cohesion of the national minority and infringes on the fundamental rights of individuals. It increasingly deprives great masses of people of doctors and nursing staff familiar with the local minority language. Such government measures are not only inhumane but also violate the professional ethics of the medical profession. We could enumerate other examples demonstrating the brutal results of this internal colonization process which results from the rapid rate of mass immigration

---

* Romanian currency, with value of 27,5 lei = 1 U.S. dollar at the end of the 1980s.

of Romanians. It worsens the opportunities in employment, education, social welfare, and other aspects of the daily existence of the minorities. They are helpless in the face of these state directed abuses.

The authorities are radically transforming the national character of the towns and sub-regions of Transylvania by controlling the geographical location of industrial investments, the creation or elimination of jobs and workplaces. There is restriction of employment opportunities and the use of a discriminatory quota system. Certain cities are "closed" to Hungarians. Hungarians also experience the deliberate manipulation of permits for resettlement, the discriminatory allocation of housing, as well as the practice of "zoning," the preferred development of some settlements and the hindering or destruction of others. The government's strategy, in short, is a dual one. On the one hand, it seeks to ensure a Romanian majority in all areas while, simultaneously, dispersing the Hungarian minority, particularly the intelligentsia, throughout the country, forcing them to move to rural areas or to remote regions having no ethnic Hungarian inhabitants. As a consequence of these policies, Hungarians are being increasingly pushed to the periphery, in both the geographical and social sense of the term.

In early 1988, the Romanian government announced a program aimed at the "systematization of settlements." Under this scheme, the government plans to liquidate some eight thousand villages on the pretext of "modernizing agriculture" and setting up new "agro-industrial centers." The authorities attribute the poor output of agriculture to the scarcity of arable land and not to the inefficient system of economic management. Their answer is to increase the area of cropland by razing "prospectless settlements" in large numbers. The radical reduction in the number of villages and the concentration of population in new settlement centers will apply to all counties. This forced relocation of population not only violates the fundamental human rights of all persons, without regard to nationality, but will also result in the destruction of local communities, architectural treasures, and ancient monuments. The destruction of the traditional settlements of Hungarians, Germans (Saxons of Transylvania and Swabians of the Banat), South Slavs (Serbs and Croats), Slovaks, Ukrainians, and other nationalities is aimed at forcibly ending their communal and cultural solidarity. The conception of "systematization of settlements" demonstrates how the most extreme measures of Hitlerian and Stalinist despotism are still employed on our continent in the 1980s. If the scheme is implemented, it is bound to obliterate even the memory of smaller nationalities and will also deal an irreparable blow to the historical and cultural identity of the large community of Transylvanian Hungarians. As a result, hundreds of settlements having a majority or a considerable number of Hungarian inhabitants will disappear from the map, particularly in Harghita, Covasna, Cluj, Bihor, Mureş, Alba (Fehér), and some other counties.[12]

Until the end of World War II, Hungarians living in the territory attached to Romania in 1920 were part of a complex and stratified society. The different classes, strata and groups, ranging from the upper middle class and the aristocracy to the proletariat and the peasantry composed a unified social order of their own. Over the past forty years, however, Hungarian society in Romania has been reduced to a bipolar social order. Standing above its bulk, which is composed of utterly pauperized masses of industrial and agricultural workers, is an ever thinner stratum of the intellectual elite. This change, which has followed the overall pattern of Romanian and East European trends, has led to a massing on a lower level. This has been an incalculable loss for the minority population because destruction of the middle strata has eliminated their most important preserver of national identity. This mutilation of the social structure has also led to a mutilated language. Hungarian language use related to different economic, technical, cultural, political, health and other activities has declined and has been replaced by the menacingly divisive dichotomy of the literary language, utilized by few, and the vernacular, which contains increasingly more foreign elements.

The 1966 census provides the latest breakdown of the Romanian population by nationality with respect to education. At that time, Hungarians in the lower school categories (and, among these, the partly Hungarian-language, specialized secondary and industrial schools) were somewhat above their proportion of the population, but they were under-represented among university and college graduates. In fact, there has been a steady decline in the ratio of Hungarians in intellectual professions since 1956. The reasons for this tendency is discrimination in university admission policies and the almost complete suppression of mother-tongue instruction in higher levels of education. Also important as a contributing factor is wholesale emigration.

The distribution of professionals also reflects manipulation by the state. While a larger proportion of Romanians than Hungarians or Germans lives in villages, the ratio of university graduates among Romanians is smaller than in the case of the other two nationalities. However, due to the above-mentioned state policy of assigning and relocating specialists, the situation in Transylvanian towns is different, there the Hungarian and German intellectuals are under-represented.[13]

A measure promoting the centrally directed weakening of the minority population is the replacement of their leading cadres. This has been going on for decades in the Romanian party and administrative organs, in economic management, and in the armed forces command. Now in the 1980s the process has sharply accelerated. This means that city and county party secretaries, leading members of people's councils, and enterprise managers of Hungarian nationality, as well as Hungarian officers in the army, police, and state security service have been replaced by persons of Romanian nationality. Romanianization among headmasters of Hungarian-language schools was drastically speeded up in the mid-1980s; between 1984 and 1987 half of the school principals of Hungarian nationality were dismissed and replaced by Romanians. Persons of Romanian nationality with no knowledge of Hungarian were appointed to head Hungarian-language cultural institutions (e.g., theaters). These events complete the trend started already in the 1950s and 1960s, which – with the merger of Hungarian and Romanian educational institutions from university level on down to the primary school – applied the rule that the head of the merged institutions must be Romanian, while his deputy might be of Hungarian nationality.[14]

The unrealistic and immoderate rates of development envisaged by Romanian economic policy, together with its obvious failure, have been harmful to the entire population of Romania, but have proved particularly detrimental to the Hungarian minority of Transylvania. The steadily deteriorating economy, grappling with difficulties encountered in exports and on the domestic market, is generating a rapid rise in unemployment. According to reliable sources, the number of unemployed in Transylvania is estimated at 300 to 400 thousand, the majority of them being 18 to 26 years of age, with Hungarians constituting a very high proportion. Owing to the shortage of energy, raw materials, and orders, the output of factories has generally declined. Consequently, under the new wage regulations, workers receive only a part of their salaries. In 1985 and 1986, in several enterprises the loss of income was compensated for by the payment of special premiums, but very few Hungarian workers received this extra allowance.[15]

The general trend of pauperization is evidenced also in the outward appearance of Transylvanian villages. Romania still lives in an era of

Stalinist-type agrarian controls. Authorities often confiscate food reserves and apply other measures to curtail production for the market. With this policy, the government creates a new administrative obstacle to those economic and human contacts which existed as a matter of course between villages and towns of Hungarian-inhabited regions. These might still exist today if circumstances were more favorable.

Chapter IV

The Political and Legal Status of the National Minorities

The General Political and Legal Setting

The legal status of Hungarians in Romania is primarily determined by two factors: the general lack of legal limitations in the political setting and the prevailing political attitude towards the Hungarian minority. Both of these factors are part of the overall strategy of ethnic assimilation.

Romania lacks genuine constitutionality. It does not rely on the principle of legality and is not committed to a governmental system under law. The Romanian Communist party plays the leading role in the codification and enforcement of law. All proposals, including draft laws, usually emanate from the party leadership. Most laws are enacted with unanimous parliamentary approval upon the recommendation of the State Council which is presided over by the secretary-general of the party. Furthermore, in the Ceausescu era more and more frequently regulation has been by presidential decrees instead of legislative acts.[16]

The general and often ambiguous wording of laws and regulations lends itself to different interpretations depending on concrete situations. Directives for their implementation are often not made public. All this gives the central and local party organs (whose heads are simultaneously leading officials of administrative agencies and the councils) a wide scope for resort to arbitrary power. Both the interpretation of legal provisions and the manner of their application is controlled by party directives. These may, and on occasion, revise the literal text of the provision in question. For this reason, many formally unrepealed laws cease to have effect in practice or, conversely, uncodified directives are strictly followed. An especially important regulatory role is played by secret directives. These are usually oral and, thus, nondocumentable sources of illegal acts and other abuses. They can be detected only indirectly through their effect. This accounts, for example, for the steady decline in the number of Hungarian and other ethnic origin students from gaining admission to universities.

A significant role is played in law enforcement by the police authorities and by *Securitate*, the state security organ. Directives of the latter are sometimes decisive in administrative decisions or judgments handed down by courts of law, especially when political importance is attached to the case in question.

It follows from the above that investigations under statutory law do not disclose much about actual legal processes and procedures. The conclusions to be drawn from them are worthy of note primarily from a historical perspective, as they enable us to track the retrograde trend of "development" from the antagonistic and contradictory, but in some respects encouraging 1945-47 period, up to the present, which is characterized by an almost total absence of rights.

The Minorities and Developments after 1945

If we consider the measures and actions taken against Hungarians and other minorities in the years following the war (such as, the setting up of internment camps, the massacres perpetrated by the "Maniu guards" in the autumn of 1944, the abuses of authority in connection with the interpretation of "alien" property, complications related to the acknowledgement of Romanian citizenship, and nationalist-oriented intrigues at various levels of public administration) as arising from the uncertainties of a transition period, then we can still single out the more characteristic trends which included certain positive legal developments.

For example, when Soviet military administration was introduced in northern Transylvania – to prevent further atrocities against the Hungarian minority – the Sanatescu government created a Ministry for National Minorities (Act 574/1944 of 14 November). Although its powers and responsibilities were not defined, it was brought into being. Under the Radescu government, the Nationality Statute (Act 86/1945 of 6 February) was codified, bringing about a fundamental change in statutory law in comparison to the inter-war period. At the same time, however, they lost the right to submit written complaints to international forums for consideration, notably to the United Nations, as had been the case in pre-war Romania. This was a new legal departure in the history of Romania. In addition to providing all citizens, regardless of race, nationality, language, and religion, with equality before the law, this new Nationality Statute also specified certain collective rights for them in a number of fields.[17]

When the Groza cabinet was formed on March 5th, 1945, and a party coalition called the National Democratic Front came into power (a development also supported by the Hungarian People's Federation, the only political organization of the Hungarian minority in post-war times), official manifestations promised a reassuring normalization of the situation of the Hungarian, German, Jewish, Serbian, Ukrainian, Slovak, and other minorities. Accordingly, in pursuance of earlier processes, Act 630/1945 of August 6th adopted certain provisions specified by the Nationality Statute.[18] For the application of the Nationality Statute and of Act 630/1945, the Council of Ministers issued laws No. 11 and 12 on September 20th, 1946. These provisions prohibited discrimination based on nationality, language, and religion and created a few fundamental institutions for the exercise of collective minority rights. These new measures dealt with the right to use one's mother tongue in private and in public life. They also specified the related duties of government offices, and the management of state and church schools for the national minorities. These institutions were to be treated on an equal footing with majority schools.

Although some elements of the above-mentioned laws represented a step back from the Nationality Statute, other developments also reflected a backing away from tolerance for diversity. The proposal of the Hungarian People's Federation for a draft law on the nationalities (July 3, 1946) was dropped. This act intended to define the rights of minorities in broader terms than the Nationality Statute had done. In spite of all this the legal provisions dating from 1945-46 made it possible for the minorities of Romania to effect some improvement in their cultural and political life. State-sponsored theaters came into existence which gave performances in Hungarian, German, and Yiddish. Mother-language schools opened for the first time for even the smallest minorities in the country, including communities like those of the Turks and Tatars. These developments reflected the inconsistencies of the political climate of the day.[19]

In spite of the atmosphere of intimidation and wide-spread election fraud, which belied democracy, the multiparty system still had a strong mass basis in the country. For the Hungarians of Romania the left wing of the Hungarian People's Federation attempted to provide guidance and representation in the country's political arena. It aligned itself with the National Democratic Front and, thus, indirectly also with the Romanian Communist party. However, in this the Hungarian People's Federation had no alternative. At that time the party press and other political manifestations of the National Peasant party and the Liberal party, reflected a violent anti-minority, anti-Hungarian attitude. Thus, the support from the Hungarian People's Federation prompted Gheorghiu-Dej, the secretary-general of the Romanian Communist party, to declare at the Central Committee meeting of July 6th, 1946, that the Hungarian population of Transylvania was an "ally of the democratic forces in the political struggle against reaction."[20]

The Nationality Statute and its related by-laws reassured both the Hungarians of Romania and public opinion abroad that there was a very good prospect in the country for finally solving the nationality problem. This prompted the Hungarian People's Federation to make a statement to the effect that it was opposed to the partitioning of Transylvania and that it was satisfied that the rights of the minority and their right to exist would be guaranteed by the strengthening of Romanian democracy. This statement was issued while the negotiation of the Hungarian-Romanian boundary question was still on the agenda of the peace conference in Paris. Thus, while the statement may not have carried much weight in the field of great-power politics, it did serve the Romanian government with support that could be invoked before both domestic and international forums.

The statement did not guarantee the establishment of democracy in Romania. A single-party system emerged after the traditional parties were destroyed, the king was forced to abdicate and the economic life of the country nationalized. Parallel to this process all autonomous organizations were liquidated which refused to bow to the central will of the Communist Party. In the case of the Hungarian minority, the first step in this direction was the purge of the leadership of the Hungarian People's Federation. Up to this point it had functioned as a relatively independent power center. Its president, Kurkó Gyárfás, was dismissed in 1947 and replaced by leaders who were "loyal" to the Party.[21]

In June 1948, the Central Committee of the Romanian Communist party announced the intensification of class struggle. For the Hungarians this led to a campaign directed primarily against their leading intellectuals. In December 1948, the Romanian Communist party, in its statement on the nationality problem, lashed out against all national minorities under one pretext or another. The Hungarians, who had been called "allies of the democratic forces" only two years earlier thus were now branded "nationalists". Several leaders of the Hungarian People's Federation were thrown into prison on trumped-up charges. Other Hungarian public figures and even religious dignitaries were also imprisoned. At the same time, large numbers of politicians, clergymen, and cultural personalities of Romanian nationality were similarly arrested in line with the general East European schedule of Stalinist political trials.

By the end of the 1940s private property and church holdings had been transferred to state ownership and Hungarian and Romanian cooperatives had been merged. This deprived the minorities of any independent economic support. In addition, their denominational schools were secularized and increasingly transformed into the state power's instruments of thought-control. The Hungarian People's Federation by this time was reduced to only a paper existence. However, the cultural institutions which were set up after 1944 continued to function; attacks on them started only later, from the 1950s onwards.

The evolution of the definition of minority rights can be traced primarily through amendments to particular articles of the constitution's text. While the three constitutions (1948, 1952, and 1965) of post-war Romania show many similarities in their provisions on nationalities, they also reflect the special historical circumstances of the times that produced them.[22]

At the time of the promulgation of the Constitution of 1948, the Nationality Statute and its few related by-laws still had legal force in practice. True, their implementation was inconsistent and incomplete. Yet it is probably for this reason that some provisions included in subsequent texts of the Constitution are not to be found in the first post-war fundamental law. There is nothing in the latter, for example, which stipulates that books, newspapers, periodicals, and theaters in minority languages should be supported or that public institutions in districts inhabited by minorities should use the languages spoken there. Another substantial difference between the Constitution of 1948 and those of 1952 and 1965 was that the former still recognized not only the right to mother-language instruction at all grade levels of education but also the right to organize instruction in the mother tongue.

The Constitution of 1952, based on the Soviet model, provided for the establishment of a Hungarian Autonomous Region, comprising ten districts of "the territory inhabited by a compact population of Székely Hungarians." Article II stated that the Statute for the Region should be drafted by its people's council. However, ultimately nothing came of it. Thus, the envisaged autonomy became nothing more than a facade that disguised the general Romanian system of subordination of local organs. After the formation of this so-called Hungarian Autonomous Region, the official use of the minority language became increasingly restricted to its territory, and simultaneously the Nationality Statute was allowed to lapse, without ever being officially revoked. At any rate, in practice it ceased to have legal effect at this time. The "autonomous" region included about one-third of Romania's Hungarian population. It became a kind of cultural ghetto, which was encouraged also by the forcible removal of a few Hungarian cultural and educational institutions from the capital of Transylvania, Cluj (Kolozsvár), and their transfer to Tîrgu-Mureş, the capital of the new autonomous region.

At its meeting of December 19th, 1960, the Central Committee of the Romanian Communist party, on the motion of Nicolae Ceausescu who was then one of the secretaries of the Committee, adopted a resolution which recommended that the Grand National Assembly redefine the administrative boundaries and the name of the Hungarian Autonomous Region. By this time even the illusion of autonomy had become unacceptable. Consequently, a few purely Hungarian districts were detached from the region, while the Romanian-inhabited districts of Sărmăs (Sármás) and Ludus (Ludas), as well as other areas, were annexed to it. This change reduced the compact Hungarian character of the population within the region and renamed it the Mureş-Maghiar Autonomous Region.[23]

The constitution presently in force, enacted by the Grand National Assembly on August 21st, 1965, has been amended several times. The most important amendment was an Act of February 17th, 1968, which put an end to the administrative division of the country into regions and introduced the county system. This also automatically eliminated the Mureş-Maghiar Autonomous region and replaced it with counties that are not identified with any nationality.

The constitution in force at present refers to the national minorities on three occasions. According to Article II, the workers of the country "without distinction for reasons of nationality, shall construct the socialist system of society."

Article XVII states:

The citizens of the Socialist Republic of Romania, irrespective of nationality, race, sex, or religion, shall enjoy identical rights in all matters concerning economic, political, legal, and social existence.

> The State shall guarantee the equality of citizens before the law. Any limitation of these rights and any discrimination in their exercise for reasons of nationality, race, sex, or religion shall be prohibited.
>
> Any manifestation aimed at introducing such limitations, as well as nationalistic-chauvinistic propaganda and incitement to racial or national hatred, shall come under the penalty of the law.[24]

What Article XVII contains over and above the pertinent provisions of the 1952 constitution is the recognition of equal rights in the legal and social sectors of life and the guarantee of equality for all citizens of the country before the law.

Specific nationality rights are defined in Article XXII of the present constitution as follows:

> Cohabiting nationalities in the Socialist Republic of Romania shall be assured of the free use of their respective mother tongues as well as access to books, newspapers, periodicals, theatres and all grades of education in their own languages. In those territorial-administrative units containing nationality populations in addition to Romanians, all decision-making agencies and institutions shall use, in speech and in writing, also the language of the respective nationality and appoint officials from its members or from among other citizens familiar with the language and manners of the local population.[25]

The above passages of the Constitution are more general than the text of the Nationality Statute. While the latter is still formally in effect, it cannot be invoked. More detailed regulation is offered by lower-level provisions of law, but only on a few insignificant points. For example, Act 57/1968 on the organization of people's councils adds to the text of the Constitution that in areas inhabited by minorities, decisions shall be made public also in the minority languages. However, the Act contains nothing regarding criteria for determining the limits of the districts where this provision is to be enforced.

Act 11/1968 also resorts to generalities. Under the terms of this law students belonging to national minorities may choose between a district school offering instruction in Romanian or in the language of their own respective nationality. With respect to the universities, the law makes no mention of the language of instruction, nor does it contain provisions regarding the language of matriculation. Act 113/1978 on public education is formulated in somewhat greater detail and recognizes the right to use the mother language, among others, in higher grades of education and also during matriculation exams.[26] The Act was promulgated in the *Buletinul Oficial* on December 26th, 1978, so that the extent of implementation can be judged on the basis of the policy pursued in the 1980s. This period has witnessed the Romanian government's most vehement and systematic attack against the cultural and educational institutions of the minorities.

Since the end of the 1940s the legal definition of minority rights has become more and more constraining. It has adjusted to an orientation that has been distinctly anti-minority. The party documents – which in recent decades have coincided with the pronouncements of the party secretary general – have played a formative role in every aspect of social and political existence. So too they have defined the legal status of minorities.

To understand the true nature of Romania's policy toward minorities it is essential to consider one of its important and intermittently recurring tactical elements. The essence of this particular tactic is that after, and often simultaneously with, repeated anti-Hungarian attacks such as the phasing out of institutions, imprisonment of minority leaders, the Romanian government usually offers some concessions which give the minority the feeling not only of having lost but also of having gained something. At the psychological moment following a loss, any concession, however transparent, is regarded by the loser as a new reprieve. As a rule, this excellently mounted offensive operation, executed with great precision, sows hope even where there are no prospects. The modest, and mostly temporary gain is upgraded in the eyes of the minority and appears as a new opportunity, especially when it follows a period of merciless persecution.

The deteriorating condition of the minorities can be illustrated by historical facts. The "nationalist" accusations levelled against Hungarians and other minorities as a collectivity in the 1950s and the imprisonment of their leaders were followed by the establishment of the Hungarian Autonomous Region.[27] The latter, at least formally, promised autonomy to the Hungarians. Also, hardly had the Hungarian People's Federation been dissolved when some of its imprisoned communist leaders – but only a few – were granted amnesty. In addition, the policy objective for "homogenizing" the Romanian nation and the ethnic minorities was temporarily put on hold, and even the Csángó (Moldavian) Hungarian schools, which were in danger of being shut down, were granted a few years of respite.

In this scheme of "switching on and off" now tightening, now loosening the political pressure, an important part was always played by the ups-and-downs of the political situation. In the show trials of the leaders of the Hungarian People's Federation and other personalities, one of the major charges in the indictment was collusion with Hungary's "Titoists," particularly László Rajk. After the 1956 revolution in Hungary, the charge of revisionism was extended to all Hungarians in Romania, and the new anti-Hungarian trials were then staged in several waves between 1957 and 1961. In 1959 they merged the Hungarian Bolyai University and the Romanian Babeş University of Cluj. Meanwhile, a party resolution confirmed, by way of compensation, that admission to university studies would be possible after matriculating in Hungarian.

In 1968, too, internal affairs became mixed with motivations of world politics (the events in Czechoslovakia, the debates about federation in Yugoslavia). It was in that same year that the Mureş-Maghiar Autonomous Region in Romania was liquidated. Simultaneously, minority grievances were dealt with at a party plenum, where the leadership promised to allow the wider use of Hungarian in schools and in cultural life. Indeed, a nationality publishing house was established, new press organs came into being, and a Hungarian-language television broadcast was launched.[28] In the first half of the 1970s, however, a reversal set in again. A new wave of coerced assimilation began, with occasional tactical compensations initially, but with no concessions since the mid-1980s.

The latest period is characterized by the enactment of overtly discriminatory legislation. This demonstrates, on the one hand, the contradictions and incoherence of Romanian lawmaking, the enforcement of norms contrary to constitutionally recognized equality before the law and, on the other, the worsening of the political status of minorities.

One such statute is the State Council's Law-decree No. 225/1974 of December 6th forbidding Romanian citizens to offer lodging to any foreigner except closest direct relatives (spouse, parents, children, and siblings).[29] The decree even prohibits accommodation at camping sites, and its breach is liable to a fine of 5 to 15 thousand lei. This legal provision is detrimental primarily to the minorities and, above all, to the Hungarians because of their high numerical ratio. Its obvious aim is to restrict personal contacts between people coming from Hungary and those in Transylvania as well as between any "mother nation" and its co-nationals that live as minorities in Romania. The discriminatory nature of this measure is evident in its modification under Decree No. 372/1976 of November 9th, according to which foreigners "of [ethnic] Romanian descent" may be put up at the home of "any of their relatives" residing in Romania.[30]

Also worth mentioning here is the State Council's Law Decree No. 402/1982 of November 1st.[31] Under this decree, persons applying for permission to settle abroad (to emigrate) are obliged to repay the costs of their education in convertible currency prior to the receipt of their passports. This decree was probably intended only for occasional diplomatic blackmail whereby through its publication and subsequent "liberal" non-application, Romania might obtain the right to preferential treatment in trade in the United States, i.e., the status of a most-favored nation. But the decree has not been revoked and its discriminatory nature is unequivocal. It is detrimental primarily to members of the German minority, who leave Romania by the tens of thousands every year. Their relatives and acquaintances abroad or in the Federal Republic of Germany must raise the required sums of money, since Romanian citizens are not permitted to possess foreign currency. Theoretically, the provision is equally applicable to Hungarians and members of other nationalities desiring to emigrate. We know of a number of cases in which university graduates who wished to settle in Hungary, but who had not yet served their compulsory three-year *stagiatura**, were required to pay the expenses of their university education, in lei, and to reimburse any scholarship grants they had received.

Law Decree No. 278/1973 on the organization of educational establishments, issued by the Romanian State Council on May 13th, 1973, is also flagrantly discriminatory, based on criteria of language and nationality. It is detrimental to all minorities. It provides that "in townships where primary schools offer instruction in the languages of cohabiting nationalities," "... sections or classes taught in Romanian shall be organized, irrespective of the number of students."[32]

The same decree also stipulates that the minimum number of children shall be at least 25 in primary school classes and 36 in secondary school classes for minorities. The maintenance of classes with fewer students is dependent on the special approval of the Ministry of Public Education. This requirement is clearly detrimental to institutions teaching in the languages of national minorities.

The above decree is the major legal justification for the Romanianization of the national minority schools. It should be noted that the operative

---

* University students, upon graduation, are required to fulfill a kind of professional internship within a civil service framework.

clause in the text is formulated not as a permissive provision but as a prescriptive rule, i.e., Romanian sections or classes shall be organized.

Political Ideology and the Minorities

Romania – together with Albania – is the last state in Europe that has preserved most of the Stalinist traditions in its political process and governmental structure. Romanian society remains in almost every detail, a totalitarian society, where the influence exercised by individuals and their various social units over public affairs is altogether insignificant.

In the late 1940s, a monolithic and centralized political structure emerged in the countries of Eastern and Central Europe. It liquidated all democratic institutions, eliminated opposition and established a monopoly of political control. The history of Romania, long-lasting Ottoman domination, Phanariot traditions and forced isolation from major European intellectual currents in modern times, explains in part why a totalitarian dictatorship has been able to survive virtually intact. In fact, it has even set the foundations for the dynastic aspirations of the Ceausescu family over the past two decades.[33] Another reason for the survival of the Stalinist system is the ability of Romanian leaders to exploit nationalism to legitimize their ends. This too is a reflection of the country's historical legacy. This strategy first proved useful in foreign policy. Later, with the general devaluation of Romania's international standing, it has come to fill more and more of an internal function as a "substitute for democracy and economic well being."

Romania's present political system is thus a peculiar mixture of Stalinist dictatorship, traditional Byzantine and Balkan style despotism, and extreme chauvinism. Romania is simultaneously an autocratic and an ethnocentric state. Its present leaders justify the prevailing poverty and oppression less and less by referring to the ongoing needs of class struggle and more and more in terms of nationalistic aspirations. In line with fascist models, their ideology defines minorities and "foreigners" in general, as a source of danger. Thus, the minority becomes an alien scapegoat. The democratically oriented elements of the different nationalities are prevented from coming together and joining forces in resistance because they are deliberately incited against each other. Divide and conquer is the tactic followed. The absence of individual and group rights, combined with police terror creates an atmosphere of fear and defenselessness. This state power penetrates all spheres of minority life.

The propagation of Romanian national supremacy and discrimination against minorities are complementary and logically related elements in nationalist ideology. In practice, however, during the past two decades the Romanian government has also made some tactical concessions to the minorities, including the Hungarians. (The rationale of this policy has been discussed above.) This was the case, for example, in the late 1960s when permission was given to set up a few minority institutions and organizations. A particularly promising development initially, from a political perspective, was the creation of the Hungarian Nationality Worker's Council – parallel with a German body bearing a similar name – as an "agency of interest representation." The members of this council were appointed by the government, usually by dint of a party resolution rather than through legal channels. During the first few years, in line with expectations, the Council discussed important matters of real concern to the minorities. In 1971, however, its representative role was eliminated. The Council did not meet for three years and its leading officials were dismissed. The members ousted from its leadership included the noted representatives of Hungarian intellectual life, such as András Sütő, Géza Domokos, Edgár Balogh, and József Méliusz. They were replaced by persons who had already established their subservience to the government's policy but who did not have either the minority's support nor did they have its interests at heart.

To this day the Council does not have its own charter, does not have membership, and lacks an administrative arm. It convenes only on rare occasions. Initially, it met once a year; later, only sporadically, at widely spaced intervals and exclusively in connection with international developments. It is a typical front organization of the Stalinist-type political system.[34] Its meetings are conducted in Romanian and only serve a demonstrative purpose. Moreover, in the Romanian-Hungarian interstate disputes of the past few years, the Romanian government has assigned the Council the disgraceful function of representing the official nationalist Romanian position concerning Hungary.[35] In its meetings, the designated speakers often have to read texts prepared for them. Those who are reluctant to do so, as happened, for example, after the Council meeting held in early 1987, are called to account at their workplace or before the authorities.[36]

The Hungarians of Transylvania are not represented in the leading policy-making bodies of the party. Those of Hungarian nationality who do occupy highly visible posts, e.g., János Fazekas and Mihály Gere, live in complete isolation from the Hungarian community and do not appear formally on the political stage as persons of Hungarian nationality. Mihály Gere's name, for example, appears in the Romanian press as "Mihai Ghere," the Romanianized variant of his name. Neither their former national community nor the secretary-general of the party who nominated them to their posts, regard these individuals as representatives of the Hungarian minority.

Those individuals who do exhibit real potential for representing the interests of their minority have all been gradually removed from leading party and government positions. In 1987, József Szász was relieved of his post as party secretary in Harghita county, which is 80% Hungarian. He was replaced by an ethnic Romanian, Aurel Costea, while Szász was transferred to Romanian-inhabited Turnu-Severin. Of all the regions inhabited by Hungarians, the party organization of Covasna county alone still has a first secretary bearing a Hungarian name, István Rab. However, he too, rates as being of Romanian nationality since in his home he communicates in Romanian with his own family. During the present decade, the number of persons of Hungarian nationality has been drastically reduced in the leading posts of the organs of central or local public administration. There are no cabinet ministers of Hungarian nationality, although three deputy ministers are still Hungarian.

In 1977, Károly Király wrote a public letter to the meeting of the CSCE (Conference on Security and Cooperation in Europe) concerning the intolerable conditions of existence of the Hungarian minority. Király's voice was heard because he had been a Hungarian who occupied important political posts in Romania during the early 1970s. Subsequently he has been subjected to relentless persecution and harassment. In his 1977 letter he pointed out, among other things, that the ethnic composition of the Grand National Assembly (Romania's parliament) was not a true reflection of the country's actual ethnic profile. Since Király's letter the underrepresentation of minorities has become even more pronounced.[37]

The armed forces (army, police, and state security service) are all traditional bastions of Romanian nationalism. The minorities are systematically excluded from leadership or even membership in them. By the middle of the 1980s, all officers of ethnic minority origin had been removed from posts of military leadership. The dismissal of lower-echelon officers is now in progress. Among senior officers of the para-military formations (Patriotic Guards, Homeland Falcons), which had been set up as organizations for civilian policing or education in the militarist and nationalist spirit, it is virtually impossible to find persons of minority origin even in those parts of the country largely inhabited by a minority population.

The state security service, *Securitate*, employs minority members only as subordinate agents and informers, but reserves upper echelons exclusively for "pure" Romanians. Only ethnic Romanians are considered loyal to the regime. The secret police play a particularly important role in the implementation of anti-minority policies. They intimidate noted personalities belonging to the minorities, employing drastic and unconstitutional means, including unlawful house searches and interrogations, which are frequent occurrences. In recent years, even criminal measures have been employed, disguised as accidents and suicides.

An additional important "responsibility" of the Romanian secret service is to spread false information in the West concerning the situation of minorities in Romania. Besides dissemination of such information and related disinformation activities, its agents attempt to obstruct resolutions condemning Romania at international forums, and hinder the cooperative efforts of democratic forces in the Romanian and Hungarian émigré communities with respect to the minorities.[38] In these activities, the Romanian government has successfully established close links with the Iron Guard[39] and other emigrant organizations of the extreme right.

There is a strong ideological affinity binding today's Romanian totalitarian regime with the earlier Iron Guard traditions as well as with contemporary intellectual trends among extreme right Romanian emigrants. A common element of their intellectual consensus is the claim that the Romanians are an ancient nation dating back thousands of years. Furthermore their civilization is superior to those of the peoples surrounding them. This view is a vulgarized version, hardened into political dogma, of the much debated Daco-Roman theory postulating a "Romanian" presence and continuity in the region. The theory dates back to the beginning of the Transylvanian Romanian national movement, and arose initially as an ideology of Romanian national aspirations in the face of Hungarian national supremacy. Today, however, it is directed mainly against the minorities, above all, against the Hungarians.[40]

The present image of Hungarians is a direct consequence of this official Romanian ideology. According to the government's official distortion, the Hungarian people arrived on Romanian soil as a conquering barbarian horde of Mongolian origin, who migrated to Transylvania in the ninth century. There they subjugated the indigenous Romanian population, a people who had originated from the intermixing of Dacians and Romans. The invaders took over many of the subjugated people's institutions and, during the thousand years that followed the conquest, they oppressed the Romanians and attempted to Hungarianize them.

In accordance with this interpretation, the Hungarians are said to have inherited their ancestors' arrogant, impetuous, and quarrelsome nature. Their present efforts to protect their cultural rights is seen as an endeavor to restore their Transylvanian dominance. They are accused of seeking more rights for themselves than the Romanians enjoy in their own ancestral lands. In their souls they are believed to secretly harbor revisionist, irredentist, and even fascist sentiments, although outwardly they pretend to be gentle and upright people. They speak of friendship, all the while waiting for their chance to take bloody revenge on the Romanians, thereby repeating their former atrocities. This is why their very presence constitutes a threat to present-day Romania. No matter where they may happen to be, Hungarian Transylvanians are believed to possess character traits and ambitions in common with their relatives and other co-nationals across the border. For this reason, all contacts between them are regarded as suspicious and potentially threatening.

The above allegations varied in form and detail are constantly elaborated upon and expanded. More and more space and time is devoted to this anti-Hungarianism in Romanian journalism and literature, in an ideologized form of historiography, and in the curriculum of public education.[41]

This anti-minority propaganda is poisoning majority-minority relations. Frequent repetition enhances the authenticity of any allegation, especially if it appeals to the vanity of the majority population to which it is addressed. Its acceptance is also facilitated by the anti-Hungarian legacy in the writings of a few formerly renowned Romanian personalities, writing in a substantially different ideological context. It is also conversely true that, since the period of national awakening, certain Hungarian cultural and political figures have similarly entertained false notions about Romanians, notions prompted by actual territorial disputes and social conflicts.

The basic problem today is that a large part of the Romanian population passively accepts the distortions based on the prevailing national ideology. The main responsibility for propagating this ideology rests with the state-monopolized information service, which makes it virtually impossible for Romanian citizens to become exposed to different views and ideas, whether originating from Romanian or Hungarian sources or from others.

The fact of the matter is that for many generations now people of different languages and denominations have been living together on Transylvanian soil. They have developed many positive forms of coexistence over the centuries. During the course of the last two centuries the development of modern nationalism has put Hungarian and Romanian ideologies on a collision course precisely over the question of territorial rights. In the tragic conflicts of the 19th and 20th centuries, both Hungarians and Romanians have experienced discrimination and deprivation of rights.

Under Ceausescu the exclusivist ideology of Romanian nationalism enjoys the full support of a totalitarian state power. In spite of this, some of the traditional Transylvanian tolerance has survived in everyday life and in many fields of human contact. Manifestations of the rudiments of human solidarity are still visible, especially in relations between those Romanians and Hungarians whose fathers and grandfathers lived side by side within the same community.

On the level of individual contact, people of different nationalities frequently help one another and cooperate in maintaining relations between colleagues, neighbors, and friends, e.g., in procuring some of the basic necessities of life difficult to obtain in Ceausescu's Romania. In more direct personal contacts, but exclusively in private, opposition is also voiced to the regime of oppression imposed upon everyone.

Personal experience clearly demonstrates that anti-Hungarian instigation least affects farmers of purely Romanian districts, who exhibit traditional Romanian hospitality and politeness towards foreigners. The indigenous Romanian population of Transylvanian towns formerly largely-inhabited by Hungarians, are likewise difficult to incite, as they are the people who have had the most contacts with Hungarians and possess direct experiences with the Hungarian people and their culture.

The xenophobic agitation exerts the strongest impact on those people who have been moved from Romanian villages into Hungarian-inhabited towns or who have recently migrated to Transylvania from the Old Kingdom* of Romania. These newcomers are the ones who are the most inclined, for reasons of livelihood, to assume the pose of privileged autochthonous inhabitants. Also strongly affected by anti-Hungarian propaganda are those young people who have recently left school and have been raised in an atmosphere of overt chauvinism. We find among the latter those who disparage, menace, and sometimes even assault, as has happened on a number of occasions in recent years, members of ethnic minorities because they forget that they "eat Romanian bread" and dare to speak Hungarian in the street and on public vehicles.[42]

In such an atmosphere it is extremely difficult to exchange words openly or even in private with Romanians concerning the situation of the Hungarian minority. The subject is taboo. Whenever the issue is raised, the Romanian response is generally confined to a rationalizing approach, with the reply that "we are all in the same boat."

Cautious answers or silence may signify either understanding or compassion which many do not dare to express. Public expressions of compassion or understanding would be tantamount to high treason. Only if a real democratic political system, which allowed for differing opinions and interests, were to be established in Romania would it be possible to find out who in fact nurses solidarity with the oppressed ethnic minorities living within the country.

Such a change may also enable members of the Hungarian minority to discover their real friends in the process of solving common problems. It will be primarily up to Romanian democratic forces to ensure that the jointly hoped for change, when it takes place, does not lead to the shattering of yet another illusion. The Hungarian and other minorities hope that democracy will bring about the long-awaited self-government and equality of rights of all peoples.

From the late 1940s onward, the Hungarians of Transylvania have not had, nor could they legally have, any independent and democratic organizations for the expression and realization of their interests. No personal

---

* Old Kingdom refers to the regions that constituted the Kingdom of Romania prior to World War I. This means mainly the territory that is referred to as the Regat, which included the regions of Wallachia, Oltenia, and Moldavia south and east of the Carpathian mountain range and the Transylvanian Alps. The union of these regions led to the establishment of Romania in 1859. The unification was firmed up by inviting the German Hohenzollern-Sigmaringen ruling family to occupy the throne of the country in 1866. From this time until 1947 Romania became a monarchy, but the "Old Kingdom" refers only to its pre-1918 territories.

opinions could be voiced at public forums concerning their situation. Over the past four decades, the resistance or protest of one or another noted intellectual (priest, poet, teacher) has found expression either in the theological exposition of some sermon or in the metaphor of a poem, and in tragic cases has even taken the form of protest suicides. The complete hopelessness and helplessness generated by the forced merger of the Hungarian university in Cluj with the local Romanian university, led to the Hungarian professors and student leaders – László Szabédi, Zoltán Csendes and his wife, and Sándor Tóth – to take their own lives.[43]

The second half of the 1970s witnessed the politization of Hungarian minority resistance to persecution and discrimination. There were some like György Lázár, a pseudonym, and others like Lajos Takáts, a former rector of the Hungarian university in Cluj, or Károly Király, a public figure and former member of the Central Committee of the Romanian Communist party who published memoranda, open letters, and situation reports in the Western press.[44] Prior to their publication, they also forwarded these protests to the party and government organs of Romania and to international human rights organizations.

In Romania today, the espousal of minority, human, and religious rights involves tremendous risks. The machinery of Romanian state terrorism and its brutal methods of intimidation and silencing have been publicized worldwide by the reports of Amnesty International; by witnesses testifying at U.S. congressional hearings dealing with the granting of most-favored-nation status; by annual reports on human rights prepared by the U.S. State Department, and by documentary accounts published by Ion Mihai Pacepa, a Romanian general of the state-security service who defected to the West.[45]

The beginning of the 1980s saw a number of young Transylvanian intellectuals (Attila Ara-Kovács, Géza Szőcs, Károly Antal Tóth, and others) start a Hungarian underground information bulletin entitled *Ellenpontok* (Counterpoints). Only nine issues appeared before its authors were arrested and expelled from Romania. These expellees moved to Hungary and other states further to the West. The short-lived *Ellenpontok*, followed by the establishment of the Hungarian Press of Transylvania, an underground news bulletin reporting on the situation of the Hungarian minority in Romania and the growing number of protest activities, including the appearance of a new samizdat publication, called *Kiáltó Szó* (Anguished Cry), all indicate a more active stage in the resistance of the minority. These actions have occurred in response to the rapid deterioration of the situation in Romania and the government's policy goal aimed at the total cultural annihilation of all minorities.

Chapter V

Minority Access to Media, Education, and Culture

The Mass Media

In a democratic country, the press, radio, and television guarantee minorities opportunities for mass communication in their own language. This helps them preserve and develop their own culture and enables them to express specific minority interests and concerns. In Romania pluralism of views is an alien concept; freedom of the press* has been virtually non-existent for Romanian citizens and their social groups since the late 1940s.[46] The Hungarian-language press, along with newspapers of other nationalities, is thus part of the state-owned monopolistic, and totally manipulated system of mass communications.[47] The number of Hungarian-language publications has declined over the past ten to fifteen years, and those that have survived, far from representing minority interests and values, are gradually becoming instruments of the government's nationalistic propaganda and policy of ethnic discrimination.[48]

The modern electronic media became widespread in Romania in the 1950s and 1960s, just at the time when the newly nationalized information services were totally centralized. Thus, the Hungarian minority in Romania first encountered the media in its centralized form and must have considered every Hungarian word broadcast by radio or television to have been a benevolent gesture on the part of the central government.

---

* Freedom of the press and its repression in Ceausescu's Romania came abruptly to an end with his overthrow in December, 1989. However, the restraints on the written media continue in a more subtle form through financial obstacles, limited access to printing presses, paper shortages, and hindrances to the effective distribution of published materials.

In the domain of the press, however, the minority experienced, after 1948-49, the adverse consequences of centralization. The overpoliticized and tedious press of the Stalinist era must have been particularly annoying for the Hungarians, since Hungarian-language journalism in Transylvania had a rich heritage of high quality during the inter-war years. The diversity of the Hungarian press of that time is illustrated by the fact that in one year of the early 1930s seven Hungarian daily papers appeared simultaneously in Oradea. By the 1950s, practically all previous press organs had disappeared, cultural and literary publications had become utterly mediocre, and local Hungarian journalism had atrophied completely.

The present day profile of the press is essentially a product of the early 1950s. A single nationwide, "official" Hungarian-language daily appears in Bucharest, while local dailies are published in certain Hungarian-inhabited administrative units (initially regions, later counties). Other papers appear for various sectors of society (youth, women, the rural population, etc.) and there are publications with cultural and literary weekly supplements as well as a few literary and professional journals with a country-wide distribution.

Over the past few decades,* a relative revival of the Hungarian media could be observed in the space of two short periods. First, there was a certain vitality in this field towards the end of the 1950s, followed by additional growth in the late 1960s when press organs were launched in the reorganized administrative units following the introduction of the county system. (New papers were started, for example, at Sfîntu-Gheorghe (Sepsiszentgyörgy) in Covasna county and at Miercurea-Ciuc (Csíkszereda) in Harghita county. In 1971, a county-wide cultural-political weekly *A Hét* (The Week), appeared in Bucharest, and Romanian television initiated a Hungarian-language program. The early 1970s also witnessed favorable trends, as Hungarian-language mass communication expanded. On Mondays, Romanian television transmitted Hungarian programs of 2.0-2.5 hours duration, and three Romanian radio stations (Bucharest, Cluj, and Tîrgu-Mureş) broadcast in Hungarian for a total of seven hours daily.

In the middle of the 1970s, a reversal took place in this area of minority policy as well. Citing economic difficulties, the government reduced the volume and circulation of periodical publications by 30-40%. This had

---

* Present decade or this decade refers to the 1980s, when the present study was first published.

devastating consequences for Hungarian newspapers. During the following few years, while Romanian newspapers grew in volume, Hungarian-language newspapers stagnated. Simultaneously with the reduction in the volume of Hungarian newspapers, was the 10-15% increase in price, twice the rate of the price increase for Romanian language publications.

In addition to the above setbacks, growing pressure was exerted to infuse the content of the Hungarian-language mass media with more of the official propaganda of state nationalism, the personality cult of the party's secretary-general, and the biased romantic presentation of Romanian history. This squeezed out the time left for cultivating the minority's cultural and historical values. During the first half of the 1980s, the situation deteriorated even further. During this time the mass media was often used by propagandists for inciting the majority against the national minorities. As the economic situation increasingly worsened, television and radio newscasts also stepped up the glorification of the secretary-general of the party and president of the republic. These stressed "the brilliant achievements of the Ceausescu era" and the greatness of Romania.

Hungarian-language news services suffered further serious losses in December, 1984. Hungarian programs were terminated on Romanian television and the Hungarian broadcasts of the Cluj and Tîrgu-Mureş radio stations were also halted. In addition, Radio Bucharest reduced the transmission time of its Hungarian programs, initially to 60, then later to 30 minutes per day. A further loss was incurred as a result of the removal of the archives, films, and tape recordings of the three dismantled studios. These contained materials of considerable value to cultural history. They were moved to some undisclosed location (e.g., the documents of the Hungarian television studio of Bucharest) or to a location with poor storage conditions (e.g., the tape collection of the Cluj studio).

In recent years, the Hungarian minority press has been publishing more and more articles translated directly from Romanian. Some papers have even become mere carbon copies of their Romanian counterparts, e.g., *Jóbarát* (Good Friend) and *Tanügyi Újság* (Educational Journal). Moreover, even the Hungarian-language press has been forced to join in the press polemics between Hungary and Romania by unquestioningly advocating the official Romanian stance. In a number of cases, leaders of the Romanian Communist Party have still been dissatisfied with the performance of newspapers and periodicals in the Hungarian community. In the mid-1980s, for example, they removed the editor-in-chief and the deputy editor of the Hungarian weekly *A Hét* (published in Bucharest). Further adverse personnel changes for Hungarian-language culture have been those imposed on the editorial staff of *Korunk* (Our Times), a time-honored sociological review published in Cluj. Some county papers have also suffered from this kind of intervention from above. Furthermore, in recent years the minority has not been in a position to issue local periodical publications, and the Hungarian-language educational press has been virtually eliminated. The circulation of Hungarian-language county newspapers has also been reduced, and the monthly review *Művelődés* (Culture) ceased publication in January of 1986.[49]

The Education of Minorities

As is evident from the foregoing, Stalinist totalitarianism introduced a singularly devastating and aggressive policy of assimilation for the Hungarians of Romania. From that time, the forced assimilation drive, which followed the political traditions of the Kingdom of Romania, was reinforced also by the objective of building a monolithic power structure. This required the liquidation of all the self-governing and autonomous units within society. These efforts faced determined opposition on the part of the system of religious, cultural and (initially) political institutions which had been established earlier by the minorities.

Hungarian public administration in northern Transylvania during the period 1940-44 (when the territory was briefly again under Hungarian control)* made it possibe for Transylvanian Hungarians to build up a set

---

* Second Vienna Award refers to the only instance in the 20th century when a territorial compromise was attempted regarding the Transylvanian question. It led to the division of the province into two parts, with the Northern two-fifths going to Hungary and the Southern three-fifths going to Romania. To avoid a conflict that would detract from plans for a Nazi *Grossraum* both the Hungarians and Romanians were pressured to submit their dispute to the Axis for an arbitral decision. Joachim von Ribbentrop of the Third Reich and Galeazzo Ciano of Mussolini's Italy rendered the decision at a meeting in Vienna on August 30, 1940. It was a real compromise, althought at the time neither Hungary nor Romania were satisfied. However, the decision returned northern Transylvania with a Hungarian plurality to Hungary, while it left southern Transylvania with a Romanian majority as part of Romania. Ribbentrop (and Hitler) supported Romania, Ciano (and Mussolini) supported Hungary. It was an arbitral agreement, whatever one may think of the arbitrators themselves.

This Vienna decision, at least in this one respect, was superior to the Treaty of Trianon, which was simply a *Diktat* of the victors over the vanquished. Through the Second Vienna award the Romanians returned to Hungary an area of 19,300 square miles with a population of 2,385,987. Its population was mixed, but it did contain a relative majority (plurality) of

of cultural institutions suited to their traditions and political maturity. After Romanian control was re-asserted, this set-up served as the basis for an institutional self-defense system for the minority. It centered around a county-wide network of mother-tongue instruction geared towards the educational and cultural needs of the Hungarian community and extended to all levels of education.

With the signing of the 1947 Peace Treaty, the international pressure ceased to ensure Romanian respect for minority rights. Shortly thereafter began the gradual liquidation of the Hungarian institutions that had just been established within the new state framework. This erosion took several decades of systematic effort on the part of the Romanian government.

Statistics in the field of education clearly reveal the gradual narrowing of instruction for minorities in the mother tongue and the sharp restriction of study opportunities for Hungarians in particular. It also resulted in undermining the organizational effectiveness of minority education. The sense of minority national identity was directly weakened by the militant Romanian nationalist bias that permeated the curricula. In this way a growing proportion of Hungarian students, who were compelled to attend Romanian language schools, could no longer become acquainted with their own Hungarian cultural traditions in the field of literature. This policy has also been followed in Hungarian nursery schools providing mother-tongue instruction by having drastically reduced their number over the past two decades, particularly in large cities and in villages with mixed populations.

Of tremendous significance for the Hungarians of Romania after 1945 was that in addition to the network of primary and secondary schools, higher education for minority students also became institutionalized. The

---

Magyars. The statistics indicate that the award also left with Hungary approximately one million Romanians. This compares favorably with the Trianon "solution" which left 1,7004,000 Magyars under Romania. As opposed to this, Romania's Magyar minority of 1,704,000 was reduced to 533,004. Territorial changes make the compromise even cleare. In this category, Hungary received the poorer half not only in terms of area, but also in regard to natural resources and industrial capacity. A direct result of this award was the establishment of Hungarian administration over northern Transylvania. This administration lasted from August 1940 to the autumn of 1944. It provided an opportunity for a brief Hungarian cultural revival.

Bolyai University, which was named after János Bolyai,* was established next to the Romanian University in Cluj. This university was the successor to the University of Kolozsvár founded by the Hungarians in 1872, which then became a Romanian university in 1918 and then reverted to Hungarian status again in 1940. Affiliated with this Hungarian-language university was the predominantly Hungarian Tîrgu-Mureş faculty of medicine and pharmacology. It later became an "independent" institution and also became more Romanianized. Additional Hungarian educational institutions in Cluj included an agricultural institute, a music conservatory, and a fine arts college. In Tîrgu Mureş, there is a theater academy and a teacher-training college. A teacher-training college was also established in Bacău to provide teachers for the Csángó** Hungarian schools that were established after 1948 in Moldavia.

As a consequence of restrictions and cutbacks, at present, instruction in the languages of minorities is confined almost exclusively to the level of primary education. However, even at this level the opportunities have been drastically reduced. From the very outset the basic plan of the Romanian government was to merge the minority schools with Romanian educational institutions. The erosion began in 1956 with primary schools. In fact, the last Hungarian school for the Csángó Hungarians was already closed down in 1958.[50] The autonomous Hungarian university in Cluj met the same fate in 1959, just as the campaign began to eliminate autonomous secondary schools. Since the middle of this decade (1980s), there has been no autonomous establishment of secondary or higher education teaching in Hungarian or any other minority language.

---

* János Bolyai was a 19th century Hungarian mathematician whose theory of parallels made a significant contribution to non-Euclidian geometry.

** Csángó (sing.) or Csángók (pl.) refers to those Hungarians who broke off from the main body of Hungarian settlements in Transylvania and crossed the Carpathians to establish new settlements in Moldavia or Bukovina. The earliest such settlements can be traced back to the 14th century although László Mikecs in *Csángók* argues that some settlement took place probably as early as the end of the 9th century. Whatever the case may be, the Csángó population, because of its long separation from the main body of Hungarians in the Carpathian basin, developed its unique culture and retained an archaic form of the Hungarian language. In more recent years urbanization and contact with industrial society has also added many Romanian words to their vocabulary. Of all the Hungarians in Romania, they have been under most pressure to assimilate with the Romanian majority. At present there are about 100,000 Csángó Hungarians in Moldavia, primarily in Bacău county.

As a result of the above campaign minority schools have been reduced to the status of sections in educational institutions for mixed nationalities. In these diluted institutions, with the assistance of internal (usually oral) directives and intimidation, minority languages have been gradually phased out. As a means to this end, the government has applied the discriminatory statute (Act 278/1978) mentioned earlier. By virtue of this act a class taught in a minority language could be opened only if at least 25 children requested it at the primary level and 36 students requested it at the secondary level. At the same time no numerical limitation existed for Romanian students. Romanian language instruction could thus be imposed even in places where national minorities constituted the majority. Where, for example, in a school with only one or two Romanian children, a Romanian class was obligatory. In other places, parents were compelled to send their children to Romanian classes "for the sake of their children's future." Still elsewhere school inspectorates were attached to different school districts to ensure a Romanian majority in the given areas. At the same time school children were forbidden from moving from one district to another. In addition, one surreptitious means of pushing minority languages further into the background has been to Romanianize instruction in a growing number of subjects taught in minority sections of educational institutions.

In the 1970s, many secondary schools providing general education were transformed into vocational training schools on the pretext of meeting the "dynamically growing needs of the national economy." This process enabled the government to manipulate new cadres and, at the same time, led to the opening of classes with instruction in minority languages, albeit primarily in trades with lower prestige. A special method of limiting vocational training for the minorities involves limiting their access to schools close to their homes. The education of skilled workers employed in the new factories of Transylvania means attending trade schools lying east of the Carpathians, since such specialized training is provided only in overwhelmingly Romanian areas.[51]

Act 6/1969 provides (in Article 1/9 of Chapter II) that, in the schools of cohabiting nationalities, education can be entrusted only to teachers familiar with the necessary languages of instruction. In 1985 and 1986, however, on the basis of an oral directive from the Ministry of Education, the schools in Harghita and Covasna counties, were compelled to accept the appointment of Romanian teachers with virtually no knowledge of

Hungarian. Both these counties are overwhelmingly Hungarian. Several of these new appointees have since demonstrated their nationalist bias against both the children and their environment.[52] This measure has been one of the most blatant attacks on mother-tongue education. In Harghita county, 86% of the children attended Hungarian sections in 1982. In 1985, 223 newly graduated teachers were posted in this county. Of these, only eight native Hungarian speakers and 191 teachers who did not speak Hungarian were assigned to the Hungarian sections. The remainder were assigned to purely Romanian sections. According to the oral directive issued on this occasion, and in sharp contrast to the statute mentioned earlier (Act 6/1969), the teachers were to provide instruction in the language with which they were most familiar. In 1985, in Covasna county, 132 non-Hungarian speaking teachers were assigned to Hungarian sections. In 1986 150 non-Hungarian speaking teachers were assigned to those sections.[53]

Until the autumn of 1986, all 23 secondary schools of Harghita county had Hungarian principals. Romanian principals were then appointed in 17 of these schools. This was also the start of the mass dismissal of Hungarian primary school principals still employed in Transylvania. This measure was the continuation of an analogous policy for relocation of teachers which had already been pursued by the Kingdom of Romania in the early 1920s.

Incentives for Romanian teachers, in the form of bonuses, to accept permanent appointments to Romanian state schools in a Hungarian environment were set up by an Act of July 26, 1924. In Transylvania, mainly the Székely region was considered to be a cultural zone requiring Romanianization. In the present totalitarian Romania, this policy, unchanging in its objectives, has resorted to even more effective tactics for promoting its strategy of assimilation. It now has at its disposal a centralized and compulsory system for assigning teachers to school districts.

In comparing this trend with the declining number of Hungarian children receiving primary and secondary education in their mother tongue, it becomes readily apparent that the Romanian government is aiming at the complete eradication of minority education as rapidly as possible.

The discriminatory application of admission to institutions of higher education has also been used to limit Hungarian access to leadership positions in Romanian society. This is accomplished by raising educational obstacles to the recruitment and training of potential Hungarian intellectuals. It utilizes discriminatory quotas for university admission of the ethnic minorities. This is a new version of *numerus clausus*.* Between 1970 and 1980, the proportion of university students of minority origin – based on official data concerning the nationality composition of the student population – ranged from 8.08% to 8.32%, while the corresponding proportion of Hungarian students for those years ranged between 5.38% and 5.80%.[54] Yet, according to the 1977 census, the proportion of all minorities was 10.9% of the population and Hungarians constituted 7.9% of the total population. However, since the census of 1977 was probably grossly distorted in favor of Romanians, even moderate estimates show the effective ratio of Hungarians to have been nearly 9.3%. This would mean that at least 12,000, rather than 7,497, Hungarian students should have been attending university daytime classes in Romania in the year 1977.

---

* *Numerus clausus* refers to a state policy of reverse affirmative action, particularly as this relates to educational opportunities. It is a phrase that was popularized in inter-war Hungary as a mechanism of discrimination against minorities who were "over represented" in some of the professions relative to their numbers in the total population (law, medicine, business, journalism) and in their share of students in higher education. The goal of *numerus clausus* was to put a ceiling on the number of students admitted to institutions of higher education from the Jewish population. The stated objective of this policy was to give the economically disadvantaged majority access to higher education. The hidden agenda of this policy was to reduce the social, cultural, economic, and political influence of the Jews. In Romania today a policy of *numerus clausus* also exists in practice against the Hungarian minority. Although no one law provides such a "ceiling" the cumulative effect of reduced access to education in their own language, limits put on admission to higher education via discriminatory tests, the elimination of the Hungarian-language university, and numerous spoken discriminatory directives, have reduced the Hungarian share of the population's professional sector and university educated sector to less than half of what the Hungarian proportion of the overall population would warrant.

Table 4

The Population of Transylvania by Ethnic Groups and Linguistic Affiliation
(official census data in thousands)

Population	1948 by mother tongue	1956 by mother tongue	1956 by nationality	1966 by mother tongue	1966 by nationality	1977 by nationality & mother tongue
Numbers (in thousands)						
Romanian	3,752	4,081	4,052	4,570	4,559	5,321
Hungarian	1,482	1,616	1,559	1,626	1,597	1,651
German	332	373	368	374	372	323
Jewish (Yiddish)	30	10	44	1	14	8
Gypsy	-	38	78	32	49	44
Other	165	114	131	117	129	153 *
Total	5,761	6,232	6,232	6,720	6,720	7,500

*Of which, 34,059 were of "other languages and nationalities."

Percentages						
Romanian	65.1	65.5	65.0	68.0	67.9	70.9
Hungarian	25.7	25.9	25.0	24.2	23.8	22.0
German	5.8	6.0	5.9	5.6	5.5	4.3
Jewish (Yiddish)	0.5	0.2	0.7	x	0.2	0.1
Gypsy	-	0.6	1.3	0.5	0.7	0.6
Other	2.9	1.8	2.1	1.7	1.9	2.1
Total	100.0	100.0	100.0	100.0	100.0	100.0

Source: *Erdély története* [A History of Transylvania] (Budapest, 1986), p. 1767.

Table 5
Changes in the Hungarian Population of Eight Major Transylvanian Cities
(official census data)

Towns	1956 Inhabitants	1956 Of which: Hungarians	1966 Inhabitants	1966 Of which: Hungarians	1977 Inhabitants	1977 Of which: Hungarians
Arad/Arad	106,460	31,850	126,000	31,000	171,110	34,300
Brassó/Brașov	123,834	22,742	163,345	27,800	257,150	34,000
Kolozsvár/Cluj	154,723	74,155	185,663	76,000	262,421	85,400
Marosvásárhely/ Tîrgu-Mureș	65,194	48,077	86,464	60,200	130,051	81,800
Nagybánya/Baia-Mare	35,920	15,322	64,535	20,600	100,992	25,300
Nagyvárad/Oradea	98,450	58,424	122,534	63,000	171,258	75,700
Szatmárnémeti/ Satu-Mare	52,096	31,204	69,763	34,500	103,612	47,600
Temesvár/Timișoara	142,257	29,968	174,243	31,000	268,785	36,200
Total	778,934	311,742	992,547	344,100	1,465,379	420,300
In percentages						
Arad/Arad		30.0		24.6		20.0
Brassó/Brașov		18.3		17.0		13.2
Kolozsvár/Cluj		47.3		41.4		32.5
Marosvásárhely/Tîrgu-Mureș		73.8		69.6		62.9
Nagybánya/Baia-Mare		42.6		31.9		25.0
Nagyvárad/Oradea		59.1		51.4		44.2
Szatmárnémeti/Satu-Mare		59.9		49.4		45.9
Temesvár/Timișoara		21.1		17.8		13.5
Total		40.0		34.8		28.7

Source: Censuses of 1956, 1966 and 1977.

Table 6
Instruction in Hungarian for Primary-Level Pupils (Grades 1-8)

Year	Total Attendance*	Taught in Hungarian**	Percentage
1976	3,019,776	171,974	5.64
1980	3,308,462	179,569	5.42
1985	3,035,209	80,806	2.66
1986	3,030,666	60,613	2.00

Source: *The data on total number of pupils was taken from the official publication *Anuarul statistic al RSR, 1986.*
**Based on non-official press releases (Hungarian Press of Transylvania).

A similar pattern of decline over the same period can be seen at the secondary school level as well. (See table 7 below).

Table 7
Instruction in Hungarian for Students of Secondary Schools

Year	Total Attendance	Taught in Hungarian	Percentage
1976	901,977	26,417	2.97
1980	979,741	28,568	2.91
1985	1,237,955	16,284	1.31
1986	1,226,927	16,073	1.31

Source: See Table 6 above.

The above data does not include information for students attending evening classes.

The discriminatory intent of Romanian policy is even more obvious if we take into account that Hungarian students completed high school in proportionally larger numbers than their proportion of the general population. At the same time the opposite was the case for Romanian students. However, the ethnic discrimination for university admission is not a new phenomenon. It was already possible to demonstrate such discriminatory intent according to the official census data of 1986. At that time, of the adult population in Romania among ethnic Hungarians, only 1.5% had university degrees while among ethnic Romanians 2.2% had university degrees.

Additional evidence of efforts to reduce the Hungarian share of higher education in Romania is discernible from the changing ethnic composition of the instructional staff at Romanian universities. At the two most important universities for Hungarians, those of Cluj-Napoca and Tîrgu-Mureş, the declining share of the Hungarian teaching staffs is presented in Tables 8 and 9.

Hungarian Cultural Institutions

What distinguishes the members of a national minority, including the Hungarians, from the Romanian majority and the other nationalities are mainly their language and culture, and the ethnic consciousness based on them. The process of modernization (urbanization and industrialization) normally leads to a reduction in the transmission of culture via traditional forces (the family, village community) and it also leads to the increased importance of formal systems of cultural transmission via public institutions. Contradicting these general trends, in recent years minority Hungarian cultural institutions in Romania have been eliminated at an accelerated rate.

In the field of Romanian book publishing, more than 200 titles appeared in Hungarian in 1980. These titles were published in a total of about 2.3 million copies. By the middle of the 1980s, both the number of titles and the number of copies published had been reduced to about one-sixth.[55] In the early years of this decade, there still were 19 Romanian publishers that also published books in Hungarian. By 1988, with only a few exceptions, this activity was confined to the Bucharest-based minority publisher Kriterion. Since then the existence of even this publishing house has been seriously threatened. Initially, the government concocted political reasons for closing it down, then in 1986 it charged the editors with economic abuses. In 1987, the managing editor of the social sciences division was fired on the basis of political charges.[56] Strict regulations were put into effect requiring that more of the works published in Hungarian, simply be translations of Romanian works. This has been done

Table 8
Ethnic Composition of the Teaching Staff at the University of Cluj-Napoca (1970/71-1980/81)

Ethnic Composition of Staff	1970/71 No.	%	1977/78 No.	%	1980/81 No.	%
Total	819	100.0	777	100.0	772	100.0
Romanians	564	68.9	586	75.4	601	77.8
Total Minority	255	31.1	191	24.6	171	22.2
Hungarians	194	23.7	148	19.0	139	18.0
Other Minorities	61	7.4	43	5.3	32	4.1

Sources:

Miklós Danos, "Egyetemi fokon" (At the university level). Interview with Dr. János Demeter, university professor and pro-rector of the Babeş-Bolyai University in Cluj, *A Hét* [The Week], July 9, 1971.

Grigore Drondore and Kovacs Iosif "Educarea lînerei generatii în spiritul unit tii si fratiei" (Education of young generations in the spirit of unity and fraternity), *Scînteia* (the Romanian Communist Party daily), June 30, 1978.

Kovács, József: "Pregatire temeinica, absolventi competenti la Universitatea 'Babeş-Bolyai' din Cluj-Napoca" (Eminently prepared students and competent graduates at Babeş-Bolyai University in Cluj Napoca). In, *Invatamîntul în limbile nationalitatilor conlocuitoare din România* (Teaching in the languages of cohabiting nationalities). (Bucureşti, 1982), p. 94.

Table 9
Ethnic Composition of the Teaching Staff at the Institute of Medicine and Pharmacology of Tîrgu Mureş (1970/71 and 1982/83)

Ethnic Composition of Staff	1970/71* No.	%	1982/83** No.	%
Total	300	100.0	277	100.0
Romanians	95	31.7	128	46.2
Total Minorities	205	68.3	149	53.8
Hungarians	182	60.7	138	49.8
Other Minorities	23	7.7	11	4.0

Sources:

A Hét (The Week), May 28, 1971.
**Új Élet* (New Life), 1983/3, p. 4.

even while the total number of Hungarian books has been reduced. A confidential internal directive prohibits Kriterion from publishing works which deal with studies on Hungarian folklore. Thus, Kriterion has had to discontinue its series of ethnographical notes and its "Source" series presenting the work of new authors. In addition, the publication of works of fundamental importance have been held up for years because they have not been given a publishing permit (e.g., Volume 5 of *Transylvanian Hungarian Etymology* and Volume 2 of the *Hungarian Literary Encyclopedia of Romania*). The regime's contempt for the minorities is further demonstrated by Kriterion's obligation to publish some unabashedly anti-Hungarian books which serve the government's nationalistic aims and policies.

The drastic reduction of popular books and specialized works on Hungarian ethnography, history, cultural history, and sociology has dealt a serious blow to Hungarian social scientists in Romania. This follows on the heels of being deprived of an independent Hungarian institutional and organizational network. Restrictions have also become wide-spread as political considerations have circumscribed literary opportunities. These and other political disadvantages affecting the minorities have prompted several authors and men of letters to emigrate to Hungary. Those who have remained behind struggle to maintain their professional integrity. Within the limitations imposed by the totalitarian order, they have lodged their own forms of protest against these repressive policies. In 1987, for example, Sándor Kányádi, the renowned Transylvanian poet, resigned in protest from the Romanian Writers' Association.[57]

Hungary has attempted to support Hungarian book publishing in Romania. Pursuant to a book-trade agreement between publishers and booksellers of the two countries, Hungary purchases Hungarian books in large quantities from Romania in order to make the publication of such books "profitable." Hungary has also undertaken to pay a growing share of the expenses of their publication. In the early 1980s this share was about 30% and has since increased even further. However, it is worth mentioning that this book-exchange agreement with Hungary has been consistently undermined by Romania. The original agreement was that Hungarian books published in Romania would be supplemented by imports from Hungary, including Hungarian classics and contemporary Hungarian literature, scientific and technical works, and encyclopedias. Such supplemental imports were already insufficient in the 1970s (see the memorandum of former university rector Lajos Takáts)[58] and have since been gradually eliminated almost completely.

Public collections, including Hungarian-related library materials dating back more than 15-20 years, are virtually inaccessible to both Romanian and foreign researchers, particularly to Hungarian scholars.[59] The priceless treasures of Catholic and Protestant church archival collections, which document the important role played by the churches in the cultural history of the minorities, are not only unused, but are wholly or partially in danger of destruction.[60] This is due, on the one hand, to an absence of qualified archivists and financial resources necessary for the upkeep and preservation of these documents. It is also due on the other hand, to a policy of willful neglect aimed at inducing a collective "amnesia" on the minority populations. This state of affairs has already led to the deterioration of numerous archival documents, which have either suffered serious damage or have been rendered totally inaccessible. The archives and library of the former Nagyvárad (Oradea) diocese, for example, have been closed. The archives of the Cluj Catholic Status (to be discussed in the following chapter on religious affairs) have also become inaccessible to the public.

In the great museums of Transylvania, every trace of the expertly displayed former exhibitions and works of art have been removed which mirrored the coexistence of the various minorities. Medieval and recent archival materials (e.g., the municipal archives of Cluj) pertaining to Hungarians, Germans, and Jews have been placed into storage and are exposed to ultimate decomposition as a result of neglect and improper care. Part of the bibliographical and archival records pertaining to the Hungarians and the other nationalities are now stored outside Transylvania.[61] The *Kájoni Codex* discovered in 1986, as well as other historically invaluable manuscripts, are now located in Bucharest. The archival materials relating to former church schools are now also being taken from the churches and added to state collections in a haphazard fashion.

The historical consciousness of Hungarians has been undermined in still another way. In recent decades Romanian historical studies have arrogated more and more of the outstanding figures of Hungarian history and culture who have been of Transylvanian origin. In this way many Romanian school texts and even some historical works translated into foreign languages, have Romanianized such prominent Hungarian figures as György Dózsa and György Rákóczi I, as well as the entire family of the latter. Even Béla Bartók has been arrogated in this way on the pretext of his collection of Romanian folk songs. All this is done consciously to undermine the historical consciousness of Hungarians in Romania and to loosen the cultural links they have with other Hungarians throughout the region.[62]

These historical claims are not an accurate reflection of Romanian national self-definition but serve the manipulative objectives of Romanian despotism. The prevailing official state nationalism is hostile not only to minority cultures but to culture in general. It restricts the education of minorities and also effectively isolates the Romanian school system from modern influences. Finally, it is also discriminatory against the minority intelligentsia because it is hostile to the role of intellectuals as a whole. It fears the historical memory and international comparative judgment of the intellectuals who represent Romanian culture in its entirety.

It is now well known that the Romanian government has not valued the preservation of the architectural heritage of Romanian national history. (The recent redevelopment of downtown Bucharest reflects this.) Such indifference is more often coupled, however, with deliberate efforts of assimilation. A case in point is the destruction of minority built structures and memorials. Hundreds of Transylvanian mansions, churches, fortresses, and historical cemetaries are in good condition, but their continued existence has become threatened during the past few decades. Architectural monuments and town sections of art-historical value (e.g., typical streets and building complexes in downtown Oradea) are destroyed under the pretext of urban development. In addition, the authorities have sometimes prevented the renovation of churches, even though the cost of such renovations would be borne by charitable contributions. (This happened in the case of three Hungarian churches – in Arcus (Árkos), Chiurus (Csomakörös), and Sfîntu-Gheorghe – all of which had been damaged by an earthquake in the early summer of 1986).[63]

Following the dissolution of the Hungarian Autonomous Region in 1968, the removal of Hungarian inscriptions (names of streets, shops, institutions) was accelerated throughout the entire area. During the 1980s, even in settlements having a Hungarian majority, street names linked to Hungarian history and culture have been Romanianized.

Transylvania's Hungarian theatrical arts, which have a fine tradition and date back to the 18th century, have been reduced to only two independent theatres, one at Cluj and the other at Timişoara. Four other theatres have Hungarian sections, those of Tîrgu-Mureş, Oradea, Sfîntu-Gheorghe, and Satu-Mare. (In 1987, the theatrical troupe of Sfîntu-Gheorghe was reduced to a section attached to the Romanian theater.) Cluj also has a Hungarian opera company, which shares the premises of the Hungarian theater. Drama training in Hungarian since 1954 has been carried out in the István Szentgyörgyi Dramatic Institute.[64] From the beginning of the 1970s, however, it, too, has been reduced to the level of a Romanian branch of drama training, and the number of students has steadily declined to a level of only 2-4 students per class in recent years. Many Hungarian actors and directors have also been leaving Romania in recent years to settle abroad, mainly in Hungary. Due to this emigration and to limitations in the supply of actors, the remaining body of theater professionals is shrinking and is composed largely of older theater veterans.

Budget cuts and anti-intellectual policies, have drastically reduced the subsidization of theaters. The Hungarian theaters have also been undermined by the nationalistically-biased distribution of the limited available funds. For example allocations for stage scenery and costumes in the Romanian National Theater of Cluj in 1987 was ten times higher than the corresponding allocations to the Hungarian theater in the same city.[65]

In addition to these unfavorable financial conditions, the state-controlled repertoire policy has increasingly hindered Hungarian theaters from fulfilling their role in the preservation and transmission of culture. A regulation requires the majority of plays produced to be contemporary Romanian works. Most Hungarian classics and all contemporary Hungarian dramatic works are banned. Moreover, in recent years for political reasons, the staging of plays by a few noted Hungarian playwrights of Romania has become next to impossible.

The government does its utmost to keep the cultural life of the minorities on the level of amateur theatricals. At the same time it deprives this popular culture activity of its original function. A glaring example is the annual festival *Cîntarea Romaniei* (We sing thee, Romania). Initially it secured a kind of amateur forum for the culture of ethnic minorities, but then in recent years it has been less and less a cultural event and more and more a political farce for diletantes of the Ceausescu cult.

Hungarian folk-dance gatherings and amateur theater groups, as well as voluntary literary, popular culture and folklore study circles, all of which mobilized thousands of young people a couple of decades ago, have been either abolished or reduced to a quasi-illegal status.[66] They are subjected to constant police surveillance and harassment. The work of rural sociologists and collectors of Hungarian folklore is impeded by the authorities whenever possible. Substantiated reports are available on these harassments. Hungarian folklore collections have been confiscated from field workers and other atrocities perpetrated against individual researchers, e.g., in the Székely region, in the vicinity of Cluj, and above all, in the Moldavian districts inhabited by the Csángó Hungarians.[67]

Chapter VI

Church-State Relations and Minority Existence

State Religious Policy

The churches are the last and still relatively independent institutions of the Hungarian minority in Romania. During the current phase of Romanianization, however, deliberate efforts have been made to weaken or to dissolve church circles, most notably those of the Roman Catholics and the Calvinists. To understand the motivations for this effort, we need to examine briefly the state's general religious policies and the present status of churches in Romania.

In its tendency toward intolerance the Stalinist regime targeted all believers including ethnic Romanians.68 The overall aim of the state was to repress religious worship, even within the private sphere, and to subordinate the ecclesiastical hierarchy to the Party's objectives. The state's relationship to minority churches was also influenced by the churches' natural antagonism to policies aimed at national exclusivism. Each individual denomination was subjected to different methods of oppression and each was subjugated to a different degree.

Ironically, of all the denominations, the oppression of Romanians belonging to the Greek Catholic (Uniate) Church is the most serious in its consequences. The Greek Catholic (Uniate) Church, numbering some 1.5 million believers, was merged by decree in 1948 with the Romanian Orthodox Church, in effect eliminating it as a separate denomination. It received a hierarchy entirely subservient to government aspirations composed of the leaders of the Romanian Orthodox Church. This political subservience is reflected in the 1948 statement given by the newly installed Patriarch, Iustinian Marina of Bucharest, who said on this occasion: "God has charged the Orthodox Church with the mission to show the way of truth to all those who believe in the approaching fulfilment of progress and socialist welfare."69 Having accepted the government's control, the Orthodox Church has been allowed to maintain its monastic communities with its extensive property holdings. Moreover, it could retain an extensive network of institutions and publications edited in both Romanian and foreign languages. At the same time, it has been allowed to maintain extensive external relations. However, the reports of Romanian émigrés and the international press, often provide details about the ordeals of both the Romanian Orthodox and the former Greek Catholic priests as well as laymen who remain faithful to the real mission of their respective churches.70

The Romanian Orthodox Church has been a loyal servant of nationalist state policy, even participating in propaganda campaigns both at home and abroad. It has taken an active role in anti-Hungarian incitement and has continued press campaigns with this objective for many years now.71 It should be noted, however, that while the Orthodox Church is regarded as the carrier of the national faith in Romania, its official political statements cannot be equated with the views of the Romanian Christian population as a whole. At the same time, in today's state of Romanian-Hungarian relations, gestures of solidarity with the Hungarian minority churches are rare.

These policies confined the Hungarian churches within the four walls of their houses of worship, depriving them of their educational and cultural institutions and of virtually all international contacts. The monastic orders, which traditionally had played a large role in education and pastoral activity, were dissolved. The work of the so-called "Status" was terminated. This had been the organ entrusted with the conduct of the economic and cultural affairs of the Roman Catholic Church. It was endowed with funds of its own and an existence that went back centuries.72 The "Status" was a typical autonomous Transylvanian institution. As an elective Catholic secular body, it had come into being when Transylvania was still an independent Protestant principality. It existed from the 16th century until after World War II. Initially, it even had some administrative Church responsibilities. Almost all of its estates, both ploughlands and forests, however, had already been expropriated under the Romanian land reform of 1921.

Of all minority denominations, only the Calvinist* and the Unitarian churches pursue a continuous but limited publishing activity today. The *Református Szemle* (Calvinist Review), is limited to 82-pages annually with a domestic circulation of 1,100. According to the government's propaganda leaflet entitled "The Calvinist Church in the Socialist Republic of Romania"[73] altogether nine self-supporting church publications appeared between 1945 and 1976. The same source also maintained that the Calvinist Church is "not concerned" with the publication of Bibles and hymnals, because it has received gift books from sister churches in the West. (In 1972, as a result of protracted negotiations, the World Reformed Alliance was able to present 20,000 Bibles to the Romanian Calvinist Church. A large part of this gift, however, did not reach the intended audience but was placed into storage. In 1984, these Bibles were then recycled into toilet paper in the Brăila paper mill. The news of this incident leaked out and provoked great international indignation).[74]

The Catholic Church has not been in a position to publish Bibles either. During the past forty years the Catholic community has been provided only with Roman Catholic wall calendars issued at Alba-Iulia (Gyulafehérvár) and Satu-Mare. In recent decades, a prayer book, a short catechism and a liturgical calendar have also been printed.

The secularization of church schools, endorsed by Article 30 of the present constitution hurts mainly the Hungarian and German minorities. It states: "The school shall be separated from the church. No denomination, congregation, or religious community shall establish or maintain educational institutions other than specialized schools for the training of the personnel of the denomination concerned."[75] Since the Orthodox Church had already given up its own schools and transferred them to state ownership at the time when Romania was still a monarchy, the vast majority of Romanians were not affected by this new constitutional provision.

The most adversely affected have been the churches of the Hungarian minority, particularly the Roman Catholic and Calvinist Churches, the two largest religious communities of this minority.

---

* In Hungary and Romania, the designation "Calvinist" and "Reformed" refers to the same denomination, hence the names are used interchangeably in Hungarian and Romanian sources.

The Hungarian Catholic Community[76]

Some three-quarters of all Roman Catholics in Romania are Hungarians. According to conservative estimates, they number more than a million today. More than 900,000 of them live in Transylvania. The majority of the remaining 100,000 are the Csángó Hungarians, who live east of the Carpathians in Moldavia. In addition to the Hungarians, members of the Roman Catholic Church in Romania include nearly 160,000 Swabians of the Banat region and some 20,000 persons of other nationalities living in the same region. It also includes nearly 150,000 members of Romanian mother tongue or nationality living in Moldavia and Bucharest. The total number of Roman Catholics in Romania is thus between 1.3 and 1.4 million.

The Church administration rests upon four dioceses dating from the 11th century. The Transylvanian diocese, with its seat in Gyulafehérvár (Alba-Iulia) was founded in A.D. 1009. It was completely incorporated into Romania in 1918. The also annexed Partium (Crisana) and Bánság (Banat) regions comprised three dioceses which extended into Hungary as well: (1) the Szatmár (Satu-Mare) diocese, which was separated from the bishopric of Eger in 1804 when the latter became an archbishopric; (2) the diocese of Nagyvárad (Oradea), which was founded in 1093; and, (3) the diocese of Csanád, reestablished at Temesvár (Timişoara) at the end of Ottoman domination. By this time it had acquired a Swabian majority.

In 1927, the Holy See concluded a concordat with the Romanian State. This concordat took into account the changed sovereignty over the three diocese. Pursuant to this agreement, the diocese of Satu-Mare was merged with the diocese of Oradea. The Transylvanian diocese was renamed the diocese of Alba-Iulia, and the Romanian part of the diocese of Csanád was renamed the diocese of Timisoara. Under the same agreement, the Bucharest bishopric, founded in 1872, was transformed into an archbishopric. The three Transylvanian Roman Catholic bishoprics with an overwhelming Hungarian majority, as well as the bishopric of Iaşi, were in this way subordinated under Bucharest. At that time the Transylvanian diocese alone registered more than 375,000 members, while the Bucharest archbishopric had only a total of 50 to 60 thousand members assigned to 26 parishes.

Apart from the changes that took place between 1940 and 1944, the above situation prevailed until 1947, when the Romanian State abrogated its agreement with the Holy See. In 1948, it then compelled the Greek Catholics to unite with the Orthodox Church. It also recognized – by virtue of the 1950 Act on Religious cults (*Legea cultalor*) – only the jurisdiction of the Alba-Iulia bishop in Transylvanian territory, thereby also reducing the status of the other three bishoprics to archdeaconries. However, the repudiation of the concordat, inadvertantly ended the Bucharest archbishopric's jurisdiction over all the dioceses in Transylvania.

The foregoing indicates the Romanian government's successful effort to reduce the weight of the minorities and their freedom of action by reducing the organizational autonomy of their churches and by conferring disproportionate influence to the Romanians belonging to the same denomination. However, these persistent attempts to subjugate Hungarian Church leadership did not succeed. The internal life of the Church remained free of direct government control.

After 1945, the state sought to enforce a statute under which it would have had a decisive say in the appointment of ecclesiastical personnel. This was challenged by Bishop Áron Márton who submitted a counter-proposal on behalf of the other three bishoprics. The negotiations were brought to a close with the arrest of Bishop Márton in 1949. This was followed by a wave of arrests and imprisonments of Church dignitaries. In the meantime, the clergy of the diocese refused to recognize the authority of ecclesiastical figures who had been illegally imposed on the diocese by the state. Áron Márton was finally set free in 1955, and he resumed leadership over his diocese. His role was not diminished by the fact that he remained under house arrest in his episcopal palace at Alba-Iulia from the autumn of 1956 to the end of 1967. Finally, in 1980, Antal Jakab, a confidential associate of Áron Márton's became his successor as Bishop of Alba-Iulia. Antal Jakab had been convicted in 1951 and kept in forced labor camps and prisons until December 1964.

All this shows that Hungarian Catholics, despite their utter defenselessness, have been able to safeguard their internal autonomy. An important consequence is that the state has barely any say in the appointment of priests and superiors. Only in personnel matters concerning nomination to posts of a juristic nature and to some institutional appointments does the government have the right to exercise the veto. Moreover, this veto is limited to a very narrow circle: the ordained personnel of the bishopric, the Theological Academy, and the officially recognized four archdeaconries, including the dioceses of Satu-Mare, Oradea, and Timişoara. Of these, the appointment of the bishop, the suffragan, and three ordained subordinates falls within the competence of the Holy See: that of the others, within the province of the Bishop of Alba-Iulia. Consequently the state's veto right is of relatively negligible value, as the state's failed efforts to impose its will in the early 1950s demonstrates. The state has not been able to nominate candidates who are considered to be acceptable to the clergy.

The Church can also act on its own in the matters of religious instruction. In this realm civil authority does not determine the language and methods of religious instruction, the use of premises, or attendance policies. In these matters, the government has had recourse only to external means of intervention, e.g., intimidation or the timing of school activities so that they conflict with the times set aside for religious instruction.

Overall, the Roman Catholic Church of the Hungarians in Romania is characterized by a strong and independent-minded clergy and hierarchy and by an intensive religious life encompassing broad strata of the faithful which also provides an important institutional framework for the use of the mother tongue. However, the Church is deprived of access to the media and lacks a church press. It is also hindered in its contacts with sister churches in Hungary and with international Church organizations.

During the decade of the 1980s, however, new state-sponsored efforts have undermined the integrity and Hungarian character of the Church. From 1982 onward, the Theological Seminary in Alba-Iulia has been under pressure to apply an arbitrary ceiling on the number of seminarians. This would drastically hamper the training of future priests. (It should be noted that there are many in Romania who would like to enter the priesthood as a vocation). In 1977, the ceiling allowed for 40 seminarians. In 1983, the number of novices admitted was only 25 and in 1985 and 1986 only 16. As a consequence of the bishop's opposition and the backing he received from the clergy, 25 novices were again admitted in 1987. At the present time, however, the ceiling remains a major difficulty for the Protestant community.

All indications are that Romanian policymakers believe that the time is ripe for eradicating the Hungarian character of the Transylvanian Catholic communities. To this end they have utilized the unresolved problems of the Greek Catholics who have refused to be integrated into the Orthodox Church and the Romanianized Csángó Hungarians who have been dispersed by industrialization and economic pressures throughout Transylvania. Both of these latter groups are Romanian in language but Catholic in denominational commitment.

The Romanian Greek Catholics, like the Ukrainian Greek Catholics have been incorporated into the Orthodox Church. However, they have not yet given up the idea of restoring their own church, and in this quest they have always been supported by the Holy See as well. After the merger of 1948, the Romanian Greek Catholics who remained loyal to their faith, simply began to frequent the Catholic churches observing Latin rites. These were predominantly the churches of Hungarian communities. They also organized religious instruction in secret, meeting illegally in private homes, and even ordained their own priests and consecrated their own bishops.

The problem of the Romanian-speaking Roman Catholics is very unlike the problem of Romanian Greek Catholics. Since the Second Vatican Council has made the national language the language of liturgy, the Romanian speaking Roman Catholics in Transylvania have also asserted their desire for Romanian-language church services. Romanian-speaking Roman Catholics number in the tens of thousands.

Romanian authorities use these two genuine concerns to generate "demands" for the use of the Romanian language in the Catholic church services of the Hungarian parishes. The Romanian authorities encourage the Greek Catholics, who far outnumber the Moldavian Roman Catholics, to demand the celebration of Mass in Romanian in the predominantly Hungarian urban parishes. They also demand the establishment of Romanian parishes by the Bishop of Alba-Iulia. Officials of the State Office for Church Affairs and state security agents continually exert pressure to this end upon the parish priests. At the same time, "representatives" of the Romanian worshipers voice their demands in petitions to the Holy See.

There is no doubt, that the appearance of Romanian-language parishes within the Alba-Iulia diocese would launch a process in the Roman Catholic Church that would threaten the Hungarian community. It would parallel the merger of educational and cultural institutions mentioned earlier. As has been pointed out, this had led in recent decades to the almost total annihilation of their ability to transmit their language and culture. In view of the political trends, it is understandable why the Hungarian Catholics of Romania fear the Romanian government's increasingly vigorous activity in the direction of church policies. They see this as the first step to Romanianize every Roman Catholic and later, at a more opportune time, to submerge the whole of Romanian Catholicism into the Orthodox community.

The object of Romanian policy is, therefore, to polarize the Hungarian Catholic community by playing off their national consciousness, as opposed to their religious identity. The tension created by forcing a choice between nation and religion is shaking both elements of identity to their very foundations. The way to avoid this conflict situation would be one in which harmony would prevail between the mission of the Church to both the interests of the Hungarian and the Romanian Catholics alike. A new system of Church organization might be the answer. It would maintain the traditional territorial principle, but would also take into consideration mother-tongue affiliation. In other words, Romanian and Hungarian language worshipers would belong to two different bishoprics. Insofar as the number of Romanian Roman Catholics in Transylvania would justify it, they should be free to found a diocese of their own. Until their number justify this they should, as a dispersed group, come under the jurisdiction of one of the Roman Catholic dioceses east or south of the Carpathians. Similarly, the Bishop of Alba-Iulia should exercise jurisdiction over the Hungarian Catholics who are dispersed and living in areas of Romania outside the Transylvanian diocese. The proposed solution is, incidentally, also in harmony with the provisions of the canonical code (cf. Canon 372, Art. 2 and Canon 518). Such an approach to the question is also timely and feasible in Romania because the repudiation of the concordat with the Holy See by the Act on Religious Cults, left the issue of the boundaries of Roman Catholic dioceses unsettled. The new arrangement could clarify the situation as concerns bilateral relations both between the Holy See and Romania and with respect to public law. (The proposed solution would not apply to the Greek Catholic Church which had been dissolved by force in 1949. Its members demand that the church be restored to its original standing.)

The Hungarian Calvinist Community[77]

The Calvinist Church concluded an agreement with the Romanian government in 1949. This agreement gives the government authorities extensive control over the internal life of the Church. The highest-ranking ecclesiastical and secular officials of the Church (bishops, chief wardens, deacons) are selected by the state from a slate of several candidates. The result is that a number of important positions have been occupied by people beholden to state power. The Calvinists are thus today more subservient to the state than the Catholics. It should be noted, however, that the local church boards which are elected by the members, still have some influence. The church boards still enjoy considerable prestige in their respective communities in spite of the state's dictatorial power to restrict their role.

The Calvinist Church in Romania today numbers some 800,000 members. Its membership is composed almost entirely of Hungarians, and its Sunday sermons and other religious services are also conducted in Hungarian. The 732 mother or parent churches, some 150 dependent or affiliated churches, and roughly 750 dispersed congregations together constitute 13 dioceses and two church districts. At the time when this report was prepared the number of local church board members was about 12,000 and the number of pastors, 680. Attendance at religious services stands at about 12% on ordinary Sundays and 23% on holidays; 30% of the confirmed members of the Church (i.e., those who can participate in Communion) regularly partake of the Lord's Supper. Compared to international data, including data in Hungary, these figures are suggestive of a rich and manifold church life.

In addition to noting the role of the local church boards with regard to ethnic preservation, it should also be mentioned that the life of the Calvinist Church is "clergy centered." This state of affairs is a matter of historical tradition and is not a necessary element of faith. However, the employment and training of "laymen" by the Church is lagging behind the times. The brunt of the work is thus borne by the pastors, although their number will dwindle by another 75 individuals over the next five years. This means that by 1992 there will actually be some 140 vacant posts for clergymen. The reason for the shortage of pastors is the imposition of discriminatory and restrictive quotas particularly since 1979. Restriction of admission to universities is a nationwide phenomenon. Similarly, the number of students admitted to the two Orthodox, as well as to the Roman Catholic and Protestant, theological seminaries is determined by the public authorities of the central government. Even the establishment of the United Protestant Theological Seminary was the consequence of forcible state intervention which resulted in the compulsory merger of the Calvinist, Lutheran, and Unitarian theological seminaries in 1949.

The limited number of admissions before 1979 was determined on the basis of perceived needs by the Church authorities. Over the preceding thirty years, the average annual number of graduates received by the Calvinist Church had been 23. The restrictive quotas since 1979 have reduced the average number to only 8.3 per year. In reality, ten admissions are now allowed, but this number is reduced by the dropout rate. It has also been affected by the fact that not a single pastor was graduated in 1986, since the four-year course was changed to a required five years. Consequently, over the course of this period, the Church has received 15 fewer graduate theologians each year. At present, the Theological Seminary in Cluj has 48 Calvinist students instead of the customary 115 to 120.

The above situation is further aggravated by another factor. In spite of the restrictive measures mentioned in earlier chapters, the number of Hungarian town-dwellers has increased in recent decades as a result of urbanization. Consequently, more than half of the Calvinists live in cities of more than 100,000 inhabitants, where only 10% of the pastors are located. The result is that there are frequently rural congregations with 150 members and huge urban congregations where 30,000 are "ministered" to by a single pastor. Given the widely dispersed location of rural congregations and the difficult transportation conditions, the small congregations cannot be merged. This makes it impossible to transfer rural pastors to urban congregations. Ideally, the urban congregations ought to be divided up and organized under the guidance of at least some 70 to 80 pastors and assistant ministers. Thus, five years hence, the shortage of clergymen will be 210 and not 140. The actual needs of the Church will be much closer to the former figure.

Smaller Religious Groups of the Minority[78]

The Unitarian Church, which has played a prominent role in Transylvanian Hungarian culture, has 80,000 members at present. It has a bishopric at Cluj, where the training of ministers takes place at the earlier-mentioned United Theological Seminary. Since the end of the last century, the Church publishes a periodical entitled *Keresztény Magvető* (Christian Disseminator.)

The *Lutherans* are a denomination of mixed nationalities, in which Germans provide the majority of believers with fewer Hungarians and some Slovaks. The number of Hungarian members in the early 1980s exceeded 30,000. They have a Hungarian-language bishopric that has its seat in Cluj.

The newer denominations (Baptists, Pentacostalists, Adventists, etc.) are mostly composed of mixed nationalities. According to church estimates, they comprise some 80,000 members at present, but constantly increasing. The state assumes a selective stance towards these smaller denominations. While there were some 60 denominations in existence in Romania before World War II, only 12 of them are now officially recognized.

The Special Hungarian and Jewish Relationship

The Jewish "nationality" in Romania obtained Romanian citizenship only after the First World War, in 1923. Even then citizenship was only granted because the more than 100,000 persons of Jewish faith living in territories annexed to Romania had already enjoyed citizenship rights in their original country of Hungary. They also had civil and human rights which had been unknown to the Jewry of Romania prior to World War I.

On the greatly expanded and newly acquired territory of Romania after 1920 there were about 800,000 Jews. As with other national minorities, the authorities resorted to various legal and political means to Romanianize them. This also affected the mass of Transylvanian Jews, who maintained their Hungarian culture and had considerable economic potential and vast international contacts.

During the early years of World War II, in 1941-42, the Romanian fascist paramilitary organization called the Iron Guard, the Cuza movement, and the army joined forces and almost entirely liquidated the barely assimilated Jewish population of the north-eastern part of Romania. This alliance also decimated their co-religionists in Southern Transylvania and in the south of Romania by forcing them to flee or by confining them in concentration camps. The Jewry of Northern Transylvania also suffered because of the collusion of the organs of Hungary's Ministry of Interior which enabled the German Nazis to deport them to the Third Reich, where most of them perished.[79]

About 90% to 93% of the Romanian Jewish population that survived the Holocaust (numbering a little over 400,000 at the end of the war) has left the country over the past 35 years. The increasingly aggressive anti-Semitism of the state and the Party, has led to their mass emigration. Since the late 1950s, the persecution of minority cultures in general and of individualism and of communal subcultures has prompted the Jews to emigrate in larger numbers. This emigration was also encouraged by the general insecurity prevailing in Romania's social, economic and political life.

The number of Jews still living in Romania is estimated to be only 22 to 28 thousand. Moreover, as stated by Chief Rabbi Moses Rosen of Romania, 65% of these are over sixty years of age. And, according to reliable estimates, those still living in Transylvania today number no more than 5,000 individuals, including about 3,000 Hungarian-speaking Jews. Those Romanian Jews who have declared themselves to be of Hungarian nationality have been targeted for double discrimination. Their fate has always been more adverse, and they have always had fewer opportunities.

Now when in certain Romanian Party circles some openly boast that within ten years Romania will become "a state free of Jews," it becomes clear even to outside observers that the past and present of Romanian anti-Semitism,[80] has been a practice drill. What has happened to the Jewish population of Romania is now becoming an increasingly likely scenario for all other minorities as well.

Chapter VII

Hungary and the Hungarians of Romania

For seven decades now the Hungarians of Transylvania have been Romanian citizens. They have been living in a social, political, demographic, and linguistic-cultural environment that differs from that of Hungary. This set of circumstances, along with the historical factors mentioned earlier, has led to the development of some distinct identity traits. Yet, what is decisive in their relationship with Hungarians living in Hungary, is not this distinct identity factor but, rather, the elements of similarity and common identity which still bind them to one another. The fact is that, in the broader linguistic, cultural, and historical sense, Transylvanian Hungarians feel themselves to be part of the Hungarian nation. The mutual attachment which they feel for one another is a natural and common relationship which exists between most national minorities and their mother nations. The minority remains a part of the whole of the original national community from which it has become separated by political developments and legal redefinitions of status. However, owing to its cultural, linguistic, and ethnic characteristics, the minority continues to be an active element of that national community.

Today's Romania, in line with its national drive for assimilation and homogenization, denies the right of minorities to dual loyalty on the basis of citizenship and nationality. The ideal of a "unified socialist Romanian nation" absorbing the minorities has become part of the official ideology. Within this context, there is no longer any room for Hungarians, or Germans, or "others" in Romania; officially there are only "Hungarian-speaking Romanians" or "Romanians of German ethnic origin." Consequently, even scholarly references to obvious historical, linguistic, and cultural links with the Hungarian nation are automatically branded as "nationalist" and even "irredentist".

Political practice parallels these ideological commitments. It also aims at isolating the Hungarians of Romania from the outside world, above all from Hungary and from other Hungarian communities within neighboring countries. Separated from its mother nation and other Hungarian cultural communities outside Romania, renders the minority defenseless against forced assimilation. Furthermore, it becomes more difficult for the minority to inform international public opinion about discriminatory acts and violations of human rights and fundamental freedoms.

The normal development of relations between a minority and its mother nation requires the openness of frontiers to all citizens, a suitable passport and visa policy, and adequate customs and currency regulations. Romania belongs to those states on the European continent which generally restrict external contacts and attempt to cut off their citizens from the influences of the outside world.[81] Romanians are permitted to travel abroad (including to Hungary) as private citizens only once every two years. (Exceptions are made rarely and then only for cases involving extraordinary individual considerations). However, the possibility for foreign travel every two years exists, in most cases, only in principle, i.e., as a formal legal right. Police authorities frequently fail to act on travel requests, often for months on end, and subject applicants (especially those desirous of going to the West or to Hungary) to gruelling interrogations, inquiring in great detail into their destination and foreign connections. In recent years, the authorities have also tried to deter men of military age from going to Hungary, by calling them up for military (mostly labor) service for several months. Those who present their request for a passport, are immediately targeted for active military service. Yet another obstacle to travel abroad is that travellers have no legal right to exchange their money for foreign currency. Furthermore, the range of commodities which can be taken out of the country and sold for money has been considerably reduced.[82]

Visits to Romania by people from Hungary and other countries have been made extremely difficult in the last decade. Every year hundreds (in 1985, more than one thousand) Hungarians possessing valid travel documents have been arbitrarily refused entry into the country by Romanian border guards.[83] Another effective way of discouraging travel into Romania (especially by Hungarians) is the imposition of long delays at border-crossing points. Visitors to Romania sometimes have to wait several hours, even entire days, to get permission to cross the border. Thus, the isolation is achieved via control over border-traffic in both directions.

With respect to customs, the routine method is now the body search by customs officials. This applies particularly to searches of Hungarians, Yugoslavs and Western travelers. Hungarian-language publications, books, periodicals, records and tape cassettes are virtually prohibited from crossing the border into Romania, although no list of such embargoed items has ever been issued. A *de facto* ban is also imposed on the importation of religious ceremonial objects and printed matter without regard to the language involved.[84] Until the middle of the 1980s, it was still possible to mail a limited number of censored periodical publications to relatives and acquaintances in Romania on a subscription basis from Hungary. All indications are that this possibility has become drastically reduced.

Newspapers from Hungary, including *Népszabadság* (People's Freedom), the central organ of the Hungarian Socialist Workers' Party, cannot be found at newsstands in Transylvanian towns.[85] As opposed to this, between the two world wars Budapest newspapers, which were often openly hostile to Romanian policies, could still be purchased in Romania.

Centrally enforced isolation is extended also to personal contacts. Its legal basis is the previously mentioned 1974 decree on accommodations. This decree has adverse consequences primarily for Hungarians and Germans and serves as a brutal reminder of existing limitations of personal freedoms in this corner of Europe.[86] Other methods are also employed to prevent Romanian citizens from contacts with Hungarians and other "foreigners." A confidential directive of 1985 requires that all employees meet foreign citizens only in a room specifically designated for this purpose on the premises of their workplace. After the meeting they must prepare a written report on the substance of their conversation. Such reporting is obligatory for all Romanians coming into contact with foreigners.[87]

The efforts to isolate institutions from relations with foreign institutions are much easier to control centrally. For example, even a formal interstate cultural agreement between Romania and Hungary, has gradually been crippled by the Romanian side. Proposals submitted by Hungarian cultural, social, religious, and economic organizations (e.g., universities, theatres, churches, enterprises to Romanian equivalents) are either nipped in the bud one after the other or terminated after some initial steps have been taken for their implementation. Leaders of Hungarian churches in Romania, for example, cannot maintain any contact with sister churches in Hungary, and even the long-established West European connections of the Calvinist and the Catholic churches in Transylvania have been restricted to a very narrow circle. The regime only allows and appoints people who enjoy its confidence, when it negotiates with foreigners on matters of religious policy and other international issues. This applies both to the leading dignitaries of both the minority churches and the Romanian majority church.

Even economic relations, regarded as neutral from the perspective of the nationality problem, come up against official obstacles. Whenever a more enduring kind of organized cooperation seems to develop between a Hungarian firm and a Romanian enterprise in the western boundary zone of Romania the relationship runs into opposition from central authorities. In a hypercentralized and basically autarkic economic system like the Romanian economy the interest of economic units in border areas excludes any independent right to external trade. If allowed any expression at all, sooner or later it is necessarily subordinated to another will, the central will, which is largely guided by political rather than economic considerations. At present, this factor essentially determines the limits of border-zone economic contacts and other institutional cooperation between Hajdú-Bihar, Békés, and Csongrád counties in Hungary and Bihor, Arad, and Timiş counties in Romania. Such cooperation has now either been terminated or been reduced to a few formal visits by top executives.

Notwithstanding the obvious complementary interests and needs of the populations of Romania and Hungary, as well as the social and diplomatic initiatives of Hungary, cultural cooperation between the two countries has sunk to an all-time low. Until the mid-1970s, Hungarian students from Romania could study at Hungarian universities at their own expense. Furthermore cultural specialists (teachers, ethnographers, historians, folklorists) could join study tours or attend extension training courses, workshops and conferences in Hungary. Today this kind of institutional cooperation has become a thing of the past. For more than fifteen years now, Hungarian educational establishments have had no scholarship holders from Romania, and for years there have been no Romanian participants in summer university programs in Hungary. In fact, Romanian Hungarians who had been invited to attend an international ethnographic conference held in Vienna in 1986 had to turn down the invitation at the last minute because they were refused the necessary travel documents. Similarly, scholarly representatives of Romanian Hungarians were prevented from attending conferences held in Hungary in 1986 for Hungarian historians and natural scientists from abroad.[88]

The Romanian government's policy of isolation aimed at forced assimilation is injurious also for the 20,000 people of the Romanian minority living in Hungary. While until the middle of the 1980s, they still had the opportunity to send students to Romanian universities, and their teachers and librarians were allowed to attend professional training in their mother tongue in Romania, this is now no longer the case. The Romanian government fears reciprocity and therefore has increasingly limited Romanians from Hungary from attending training opportunities in Romania.

In 1977, a summit meeting was held in Debrecen and Oradea between Hungary and Romania. The Romanians signed at this time a series of agreements which might have promoted the development of better cultural-educational relations. Most of these plans, however, have failed to materialize because of lack of good faith. For example, Romania does not intend to fulfill the proposal for Hungarian and Romanian cultural institutes in the two capitals. These were to engage in the selling and lending of books and periodicals. Romania's rigid stand on this proposal has stalled the simultaneous opening of the two cultural institutes to the present.

Since the Romanian government strives to bar Hungarian access to outside printed Hungarian materials and personal contacts with foreigners it has also reduced the avenues for the institutional preservation of Hungarian culture in Romania. This dramatically reduced access has enhanced the role of Hungarian television and foreign (both Hungarian and Western) radio programs. These play an important role in upgrading public information in the mother tongue and in providing for the cultural needs of the minority. However, the opportunities for receiving such broadcasts are limited by distance and geography in a lot of places. Those viewing or listening to them are furthermore branded as disloyal citizens by authorities.[89] A typical example of official efforts to block broadcasts in recent years was the removal of receiving antennas from homes at Zalău (Zilah). These aerials were removed because they were capable of receiving television transmissions from Budapest.

Romanian authorities also endeavor to hinder individual channels of communication between the minority and Hungary via postal censorship and the refusal to construct direct, long-distance telephone links between Romania and Hungary. Both countries already have established such communication links with most other European countries. In the final analysis, however, long distance calls are a possibility for Romanian citizens only in principle. The rules in force allow calls to foreign countries only once every three months and those who infringe this rule are obligated to pay a punitive extra charge.

The Romanian government holds the Hungarian minority hostage. It is a means to blackmail the Hungarian government in their interstate relations. The character and timing of each anti-minority measure leaves no doubt that it was intended to be an unfriendly gesture towards Hungary. On the eve of April 4, 1988, Hungary's national holiday, for example, the Romanian government decreed that henceforth the minority publications must print all place-names only in their Romanian form. This provision is not only anti-Hungarian in nature but it also discriminated against publications issued in German, Serbo-Croatian, and other minority languages.[90]

As a result of the above and other aforementioned restrictions, contacts between Hungarians in Romania and in Hungary have fallen to an all time low. In the Hungarian-Romanian border zone area, this regression is incontrovertible, even in comparison with the far from ideal conditions that prevailed during the inter-war period.[91] If we compare the inter-war regulations in force concerning frontier traffic of both private persons and printed publications with the present-day situation, we can clearly note degeneration. The contrast is even sharper if we take as the basis for comparison the promising developments in Hungarian-Romanian relations that took place for a couple of years following World War II. Aside from a short period of improvement in the late 1960s (also reflected in the external relations of the minorities) Romanian policy towards the nationalities grew more oppressive. At present that slight improvement now lives only in memory and cannot be freely discussed in Romania.

These deliberate efforts to reduce relations between the Hungarian minority and their co-nationals in Hungary contravenes the basic norms of international law. It also violates the obligations which Romania has accepted in various general and regional conventions or declarations, among them in the Final Act of the Conference on Security and Cooperation in Europe. Thus, when we see the need for fundamental changes in the situation of Romania's Hungarians with respect to their external relations, we are comparing it not only to positive European examples of relations between minorities and their mother nations (ranging from international conventions concluded after 1945 for the protection of minorities, e.g., between Italy and Austria, Denmark and West Germany, Great Britain and Ireland), but to specific agreements on cultural cooperation and other matters (e.g., the Hungarian-Yugoslavian agreement on cultural cooperation and direct border-zone contacts). Romania's policy of isolating its citizens, above all its minority citizens, from the outside world violates the principles of civilized behavior in the relations between states. This policy and its objectives must be resolutely countered by Hungary and all other state signatories of the Helsinki Final Act. The various sectors of Hungarian society and all international democratic forces must also stand united against these abuses.

The rapid deterioration of the minority's situation raises the question of Hungary's responsibility for its co-nationals in Romania. After World War II, people in Hungary were hopeful and looked forward to real improvements in the situation of the Hungarian minority in Romania. By signing the Paris Peace Treaty, Hungary officially broke with all forms of irredentism. Leaders and official institutions of the two neighboring states repeatedly emphasized that a radical improvement had begun in Romanian-Hungarian relations. In this improvement they expected the Hungarian people of Transylvania to play an important role in the positive development of relations between the two countries. During those years, it appeared the two peoples had finally put behind them the suffering and the tragedies. However, the subsequent era of Stalinism gave rise not only to the nationalization and centralization of society, the economy, and culture but also to an ingrained intolerance toward the various minorities. It also led to an unprecedented antagonism between the countries concerned. This period witnessed an intensity of antagonism that had been inconceivable earlier. In this time of perpetual hostility between the two states, during the period from 1949 to 1955, even personal contacts were broken and citizens were barred from visiting each other's country.

The question of Hungarians living in neighboring countries was declared taboo by Hungary's political leaders during the Rákosi era. This stance was also encouraged by the prevailing viewpoint regarding international law and politics which, after World War II, submerged minority rights into the category of universal human rights. This relegated the matter of minorities, with few exceptions, to the exclusive domestic jurisdiction of individual states. From the end of the 1940s, the Marxian interpretation of internationalism in Hungary reckoned less and less with the nationalities, and regarded even the mere existence of Hungarians beyond the borders as nationalistic pleadings. Consequently, the issue of Hungarians living in neighboring countries became a topic about which it was inadvisable to speak in public.[92] In their criticism of earlier Hungarian nationalism and irredentism, Hungary's Stalinist ideologues and propagandists frequently adopted the anti-Hungarian arguments of the nationalists in the neighboring countries.

Not even after 1956 did the opportunity present itself for establishing contacts between Hungarians living on both sides of the border. Nor was it possible to inform public opinion in Hungary about the life and culture of Hungarians in Romania. The basically unaltered official position was that Hungary had nothing to do with the Hungarians of neighboring countries. Accordingly, press and educational establishments also remained silent about the issue. Even the sports celebrities and artists who were ethnic Hungarians had their names printed in the Hungarian press according to the rules of Romanian spelling (e.g., Iolanda Balas, Stefan Ruha), and Budapest newspapers employed the Romanian designation for centuries-old Hungarian settlements and towns of Transylvania. Terms relating to the nationality problem were simply omitted from the vocabulary of Hungarian politics and ideology. In a manner unique to Central Europe, the criticism of nationalism was focused only on the castigation of Hungarian nationalism.[93] The unfavorable consequences of such an extremely negative and one-sided image of Hungarians were that it made it difficult for a healthy self-criticism to evolve in Hungary and also conserved fallacious views and misinformation. At the same time, this excused and even indirectly encouraged the anti-Hungarian nationalism in some of the neighboring countries.

During the course of his 1958 state visit to Romania, János Kádár declared in Tîrgu-Mureş, the chief town of the still existing Hungarian Autonomous Region, that Hungary had no territorial claims against Romania. However, he failed to voice Hungary's concern for the ethnic survival of Hungarians in Romania. In fact, when in 1962 a few Hungarian intellectuals protested at international forums against the merger of the Hungarian and Romanian universities of Cluj, the protesters were found guilty of violating state interests by a court of law in Budapest.[94]

The increased tourist traffic between countries of Eastern Europe in the early 1960s made it easier to strengthen family relations and friendship ties between Hungarians living in Romania and Hungary. Still, the existence of the more than two million strong Hungarian minority in Romania remained a taboo topic in Hungarian public discussions. Representatives of official (mainly cultural) policy manifest not only indifference but vehement opposition to any consideration of the problem. In the early 1970s, a political journalist even wrote that the relationship of Hungary and Transylvania resembled the relationship between France and Algeria, as if the former were a form of colonial dependence.

From the middle of the 1960s, on behalf of Hungarian literature, a number of Hungarian writers demanded that more attention should be devoted to the Hungarian culture of Romania. Initial progress was made in this area in some literary reviews, which from time to time published the writings by Hungarian authors of Romania. In March 1968, the literary criticism section of the Hungarian Writers' Association formulated its view on Hungarian literature abroad. It pointed out that responsibility for such literature rested with both their own country and with the representatives of Hungarian literature in general. In other words, that they had dual loyalties. In addition, there was a gradual increase in the number of sociological publications concerning Hungarians outside Hungary (including Romania), although initially such publications appeared as individual ventures and not as works sanctioned for researchers affiliated with some institution.[95]

During the above period, an official reassessment began in Hungary regarding the problems of inter-ethnic and inter-nationality relations. A change in official policy can be noted from 1969, when a working group of the Central Committee of the Hungarian Socialist Workers' Party recognized, in an unpublished position paper, that cultural relations must be developed with Hungarians living in the neighboring countries. Like it or not, the numerical size of Hungarian minorities, running into the millions, demanded the attention of Hungary.

In the 1970s, Hungary gradually incorporated into its official foreign policy statements the role of national minorities as bridges uniting different peoples.[96] The Hungarian press also began to publish more reports on the life of Hungarians in Romania. In their public statements at home and abroad, responsible statesmen sometimes broached this matter as a problem. While they recognized that it was essentially within the domestic jurisdiction of Romania, they also pointed out that Romania's policies in this area would have an effect on Hungary. After all a considerable part of Hungary's population had relatives living across the border in Romania.

Nevertheless, during the 1970s and even into the 1980s, official Hungarian policy still reflected a great deal of hesitancy and uncertainty. It did not develop consistent principles on this issue and failed to formulate possible courses of action. Measures that were taken were often of an *ad hoc* nature. Furthermore, those who demanded a more assertive policy were often regarded with suspicion.[97] Moreover, young people who regularly traveled to Transylvania faced the prospects of harassment by the authorities.

Hungarian diplomacy began to be more clearly defined around the middle of the 1980's as evidenced by Hungarian representatives calling for the safeguarding of minority rights on an international level at international conferences and meetings.[98] A statement by Mátyás Szűrös, the Secretary for International Affairs of the HSWP Central Committee in January, 1988, marked an important new development. The statement referred to the Hungarian minorities living in the Carpathian basin as part of the Hungarian nation. It also outlined some elements of a more coherent Hungarian policy toward the minorities.[99] A publication issued by Imre Szokai and Csaba Tabajdi (leading officials of the foreign affairs department of the HSWP), in February, 1988, asserted in still more detail the principles and practices of the new Hungarian policy concerning the matter of the minority question.[100]

Chapter VIII

Emigrants, Immigrants, and Refugees

Historical experience shows that mass demographic movements (population exchanges, mass expulsions, exodus) have not provided a solution in this region to the problems of either the interested states or the national and ethnic communities within them. While we recognize this fact, we cannot condemn the individuals who emigrate voluntarily particularly if their condition has become unbearable or if they face serious danger because of their minority status. In the present century, the third wave of emigration from Romania has now reached Hungary.

The first exodus took place in the period following World War I when, according to the records of the National Refugee Office, some 197,000 Hungarians fled from Romania between 1918 and 1924. They were followed by an additional 169,000 refugees emigrating to Hungary at a slower rate between 1924 and 1940.[101] Of the above the largest number of Hungarians left Romania during the eighteen months between the end of the war and the signing of the Treaty of Trianon. At that time the fate of Transylvania and the legal status of its Hungarian nationality were still uncertain.

Hardly had a generation passed, during which the experiences of the first exodus still lived in the collective memory, when the Vienna Award of 1940 reannexed northern Transylvania to Hungary, leaving southern Transylvania as part of Romania.* Neither of the two regions was ethnically homogeneous, and in the days following the Vienna decision thousands of Romanians and Hungarians left the divided Transylvanian territories in order to establish themselves in their mother country or in a region contiguous with it. Between 1940 and 1944, about 200,000 Hungarians

---

* See note on Second Vienna Award, p. 62.

migrated to Hungary and to northern Transylvania. They fled from intensifying persecution and the foreseeable oppression from the Romanian administration which they had experienced during the past 22 years.[102] Many of the first wave refugees who had earlier emigrated to Hungary now chose to return to their former home in Transylvania. After World War II, some of them remained permanent residents of Transylvania, which now again came under Romanian rule. Others joined the hundred thousand or so refugees fleeing once more towards Hungary and the West. The present period is witnessing the peak of the third wave of emigration.

Romania's current actual emigration policy seems to contradict its stated principles. One of Romania's primary objectives is to encourage population increase by any means. Official demographic policy tries to limit would-be emigrants in general.

The International Covenant on Civil and Political Rights signed by Romania in 1974 provides in Article 12 that: "Everyone shall be free to leave any country, including his own."[103] Yet, emigration is strictly limited in Romania. Those applying for permission to emigrate face immediate dismissal from their jobs, as well as harassment and, occasionally, imprisonment. According to Amnesty International's July 1987 report on Romania, hundreds of people have been imprisoned for seeking to exercise their right to leave the country.[104]

The Romanian criminal code, which runs counter to the international covenant signed by Romania, stipulates in Article 245 that any plan or intention to illegally cross the border qualifies as an attempted border-crossing and the perpetrator is liable to imprisonment from six months to three years. In the majority of the cases known to Amnesty International, persons who attempted to cross the border illegally were those who had earlier been harassed because of their religious, ideological, or political convictions. For this reason Amnesty International recognizes them as political prisoners and takes them under its protection.[105]

Romanian border guards have, on numerous occasions, shot down people attempting to flee across the border. On May 29, 1987, for example, 28-year-old Lionte Gheorghe was shot dead on Hungarian territory by a Romanian soldier who pursued him across the border. Several such deaths have also been reported on the border between Romania and Yugoslavia. All this, however, does not deter those who are determined to leave the country. In 1986, according to some Bucharest sources, the number of unanswered applications for emigration was more than 70,000. Yet another source dating from 1985 reported about a million and a half such applications.[106]

Romanian policy towards those wishing to exercise their right to leave the country is not uniform. The motto employed earlier by the Iron Guard "Romania without Jews and Magyars!" (Vrem Romania fara unguri si fara jidani!) has now been simplified to *A Romanian Romania!*. Applications for emigration by minorities living in Romania are considered on the basis of different criteria. Jewish and German applicants fall under one category and Hungarians under another.

In 1930 the Jews comprised 5% of the Romanian population. This proportion was greatly reduced by the Holocaust, and the numbers of the survivors were reduced even further by officially supported emigration. This exodus is now coming to an end. In a country where anti-Semitism has deep historical roots, the government wants to expedite the emigration of the small Jewish community in Romania for two reasons. On the one hand, the ideal of a "Romanian Romania" will come closer to being realized; on the other, the "head money" paid by Israel (and by the Federal Republic of Germany) for each Jewish emigrant constitutes a special source of income for the Romanian state.[107]

In 1930, there were 760,687 Germans in Romania. Over the course of half a century their number has been drastically decreased. The census data of 1977 shows that they have been reduced to 332,000 by that year.[108] During the present decade, about 15 thousand Germans have been leaving Romania legally every year. Under an unofficial agreement, for permission to leave Romania, the Federal Republic of Germany pays DM 10,000 for an active adult, DM 6,000 for an old-age pensioner, and DM 4,000 for a child.[109] According to international press sources, Israel pays $5,000 for a university graduate and $2,500 for a Romanian Jew having completed a course of vocational training.[110]

The number of those leaving the country legally has demonstrably increased under U.S. pressure, since the granting of most-favored-nation status to Romania was made subject to the promotion of emigration. In accordance with its ideology envisaging a homogeneous state entirely Romanian in both language and nationality, the nationalist regime is interested in seeing that the various minorities leave the country. This solution is not feasible in the case of Hungarians because they constitute a significant proportion of the total population. However, one of the sophisticated measures of denationalization is the promotion of selective emigration. While, for example, the very intention of emigrating leads to serious retaliation for the average person, in January, 1986, a prominent representative of the Hungarians of Transylvania, Géza Szőcs, was told by the police that "his safety could not be ensured" any longer, and that "it would be better" for him to leave the country.[111] In the case of persons of distinction, expulsion from the country has proven expedient. This is another disguised method which aims at the complete elimination of the intelligentsia, the leaders of the minorities. Since the middle of 1985, some Hungarians of Romania have found ways to flee to the West through Hungary. Later, following the closing of the Austrian border, most remained in Hungary, since the Hungarian authorities did not compel them to return to Romania when their passports expired. Although ostensibly the Romanian authorities do not approve of emigration, during this period they have issued passports in large numbers to intellectuals whom, in many cases, they had earlier denied the right to go abroad. In this way they have virtually encouraged them to leave.

Conscious selectivity is also demonstrated by the fact that ethnic Romanians who also flee in equally large numbers (many Romanian families are now seeking to settle in Hungary), encounter more difficulty in obtaining the necessary passport. Most likely this is also influenced by the forms of flight. It varies from one social stratum to another, with intellectuals possessing a passport and choosing the legal emigration route, while desperate and helpless lower-strata individuals are more apt to resort to illegal border crossings.

Since neither the Romanian nor the Hungarian government publishes regular statistics on emigration and immigration, we can only rely upon occasional ad hoc revelations and estimates based on them.

According to an official Hungarian statement of January 28, 1988, the number of applications for resettlement received from persons residing in Romania was 1,709 in 1985, 3,284 in 1986, and 6,499 in 1987. About 80% of these requests have been granted. Thus, the total number of immigrants from Romania increased by more than 50% in 1987. Over a period of five years, Hungary received 17,000 applications for resettlement, 91% of them from people living in neighboring countries, including more than 40% from Romania. On the other hand, the number of registered immigrants is now 25,000, i.e., 8,000 more than the number of applicants.[112]

According to the spokesman for the Hungarian government, those who emigrated from Romania in the past few years did so for reasons of family reunification. (Repatriation, i.e., the "homecoming" of persons born in

Hungary virtually came to an end as far back as 1979).[113] In most cases, family reunification disguises nominal marriage, although the number of those resorting to this tactic is on the decrease. Until quite recently the situation of immigrants, except for those receiving special privileges from the Hungarian authorities, has not been satisfactory. Up until early 1988, they were not assisted in their social and economic adjustment by any official institution, organization, or welfare agency. Instead, they were left to manage on their own in a country grappling with inflation and a serious housing shortage. Consequently, these immigrants were given a mixed reception by society, which has not always been characterized by solidarity. To complicate matters, the majority of those arriving in Hungary are intellectuals. They have fled from cultural degradation, spurred by the desire to provide a more tolerant setting for their children's future.

From June 1985 to October 28, 1986, persons in possession of Romanian passports were allowed to proceed on to Austria by Hungarian border guards. Until quite recently, Austrian refugee authorities also processed Romanian refugees rapidly and efficiently. However, it is not known what destinations they have been directed to and in what numbers.

Romanians and Hungarians of Romania have attempted to leave for the West across the Yugoslav-Hungarian border. This proved a feasible route for a few months in the summer of 1987. Those who were successful placed themselves under the protection of the Belgrade Office of the United Nations High Commissioner for Refugees. Those who failed to reach this destination were expelled by the Yugoslavian authorities.

A third avenue of escape is possible because Sweden does not require visas. A Swedish airline ticket sent by mail or purchased with foreign currency in Budapest enables its holder to travel to the West. This escape route has been resorted to by many, mainly with the aid of Hungarians living in Sweden.

An ever growing number of people are staying in Hungary illegally, without official documents and without a valid passport. These are people who have either not succeeded in continuing on to other destinations or whose original intention was to remain in Hungary. Many of these people do not wish to continue on to the West even if they were in a position to do so. Among the most emphatic reasons given for their having come to Hungary are the increasing ruthless oppression and the hopeless economic situation in Romania. Until late 1987 it was somewhat easier for these people to find employment in the second economy. A more difficult problem is to obtain a fictitious declaration of sponsorship by a family and the acquisition of a real home. The new tax regulation of 1988 has also made it more difficult to provide work opportunities for these people. Since early 1988, however, the Hungarian authorities have been issuing work permits to them in increasing numbers.

The only authority dealing with foreigners in Hungary has thus far been KEOKH, the Aliens Registration Office of the Ministry of the Interior. In many cases, it has prolonged the residence permits of those who stay in Hungary when their passport has expired. At the end of December 1987, for 160 Romanian citizens residing in Hungary, it stamped into their passports a short-term "exit permit for one occasion" valid at Romanian border stations. At the same time it cancelled the residence permits of several others, which was tantamount to an expulsion order. As far as is known, twelve of the individuals dealt with in this manner returned to Romania and nothing is known about their fate as yet. Refugees apprehended at the border by Romanian authorities are sent to a labor camp allegedly set up near Timișoara. Two refugees – four, according to another source – were beaten to death by the militia recently.[114]

Hungarian public opinion responded to the news of the expulsions with letters of protest. In letters addressed to the Prime Minister, some raised their voices against the occurrences and expressed the hope that Hungarian society would embrace the cause of those in hiding and will help them find refuge in Hungary. The harsh measures were deemed an abuse of official authority, and the responsible officials of KEOKH were relieved of their posts.

Until recently Hungarian society has lacked private efforts to address social problems. The influx of refugees has spurred the emergence of spontaneous non-governmental organizations to assist the rapidly increasing number of refugees. These newly established charitable organizations as well as initiatives on the part of private individuals and various church groups emerged around the end of 1987 and beginning of 1988. Clergymen and laymen representing the Lutheran, Calvinist, Catholic, and other denominations have tried, to the best of their abilities, to promote in an organized manner the housing of refugees and the provision of food and clothing for them. The churches have also assisted the refugees in solving the problems of resettlement and integration into Hungarian society.[115] A non-governmental social agency, the Asylum Committee, was established in January 1988. It has called on the Hungarian government and Hungarian society, as well as foreign countries to assist them in addressing the Romanian refugee problem. They have tried to coordinate the efforts of all countries in the path of the exodus from Romania.[116] To this end the Committee has already taken the first step to help the refugees.

At the same time, on the governmental level, the chairman of the National Assembly's Foreign Affairs Committee has reiterated that necessary measures will be taken to normalize the situation of those possessing valid travel documents who wish to remain in Hungary. The Hungarian government has appropriated 300 million forints establishing a special fund to provide relief for immigrants. An interdepartmental committee has also been formed to deal with the affairs of foreign citizens desiring to resettle in Hungary. Furthermore the Hungarian Red Cross is taking on an ever growing share of the implementation of assistance programs.[117] While the Hungarian government seeks to solve the problem primarily through its own efforts, it does not rule out support from abroad as well.

* * *

The ever-growing number of Hungarian refugees fleeing from Romania lays before us bewildering examples of the drama of an entire ethnic community's struggle for survival. The Hungarians of Romania live under the double pressure of political and national oppression enforced by an anti-democratic system enslaved by its own extremism. This explains the absurdity – at the end of the 20th century – that people who have lived in their own homeland for more than a thousand years are now facing, in that land the prospects of inevitable emigration or forced assimilation. The more than two million Hungarians of Romania, taken as a whole, do not have the option to emigrate but neither do they want to be assimilated. These two considerations lead to one positive certainty: that the chauvinistic state policy of Romania cannot, for a foreseeable future liquidate the ethnic communities by the methods described above. Their collective existence, nonetheless, is in much greater danger today than at any time in past history. They are unable to control their own destiny or to envisage any future. They are exposed to the despotism of an extreme nationalist dictatorship reminiscent of fascism in both its attitudes and methods. In such a situation, the Hungarians of Romania can expect assistance only from outsiders, from Hungary and Hungarian society, from the collectivity of European states which have defined the values of law and humanity in a joint declaration, and from all democratic governments and social and intellectual forces ready and able to act in their interest.

One must not forget that the present mass exodus is only a symptom of the general political ills of Romania. Only by removing these ills can Romania change in the direction of democracy. The interests of Romanian, Hungarian, and other Central and East European democratic forces coincide in the promotion of such a development.

The critical change in the situation of the Hungarian minority of Romania also draws attention to the pressing tasks facing the Hungarian State and Hungarian society. In accordance with its actul national interests and in line with the norms of international law, Hungary must act decisively and with resolve to defend the Hungarian minority under attack. Systematic solicitude for the Hungarian minority must become part of a comprehensive national strategy, which only an increasingly democratic and renewed Hungary will be able to sustain with success on the international level. The meetings of the Hungarian Democratic Forum,[118] as well as other non-governmental initiatives on the part of citizens, have recently demonstrated that different groups and institutions of Hungarian society seek an active and autonomous role in defending the interests of minorities.

The ongoing annihilation of the Hungarian minority's culture in Romania represents a deliberate refutation of the universal human values forged by the community of nations over the centuries. The authors of this study acknowledge with gratitude the stand taken in the past few years by important international forums, significant national-political institutions, as well as prominent leaders in many parts of the world, against the policies that have led to the tragic human rights violations in Romania. In situations such as this, responsibility must rest with mankind as a whole. The tragic historical examples of our own century amply demonstrate that this responsibility cannot and must not be declined by referring to the exclusive domestic jurisdiction of the concerned state. The fate of minorities within the borders of any state are no longer simply a domestic concern. In the context of global interdependence their fate has become a common concern!

In the days to come, the need for mobilizing Hungarian and international public opinion will, in all probability, become even greater. The extreme jeopardy of the ethnic Hungarians in Romania demands our attention and organizational commitment.

Chronology

The Ceausescu era's nationality policies are a consequence mainly of developments since World War II. However, the relations between Romanians and Hungarians go back at least eight hundred years and maybe even further. Therefore, the events of the major developments in Transylvanian history will be summed up in three steps. First, by reviewing the major phases in inter-ethnic and internationality relations to the 20th century. Second, by providing a summary chronology of the period from World War I to World War II. Finally by providing a detailed chronology from the end of World War II to the overthrow of Nicolae Ceausescu.

The contested region of Transylvania has been inhabited by humans for at least 140,000 years according to the findings of archeologists. These peoples have not left behind any clues regarding the language they spoke or the "ethnic" affiliation that they professed. Only in the second century B.C. do we begin to encounter people in this region who can be associated at least with some historically identifiable peoples. In this context the region is successively occupied by Sarmatians, Dacians, Romans, Goths, Alans, Huns, Bulgars, Avars. None of these peoples could maintain a lasting hold over the region. Only the arrival of the Magyars (Hungarians) in 896 A.D. set a foundation for a stable and settled occupation of the region. By the reign of (Saint) Stephen I (1000-1038) Transylvania became an important component of the medieval Hungarian Kingdom. It remained in this status for the next 500 years until the Ottoman Turkish invasion of 1526-40. At that time the Hungarian Kingdom broke into three parts, with the western part (Transdanubia and part of northern Hungary) coming under Habsburg control, while the central lowlands became an Ottorman Pashalik governed from Buda, leaving only the eastern parts (Partium and Transylvania) under the reign of Hungarian princes (mainly the Báthory and Rákóczi families). This condition lasted until the end of the 17th century (1691) when the retreat of the Ottoman Turks enabled the Habsburgs to extend their control over both the central plains and the region of Transylvania. This control was briefly interrupted in 1848-49 when the Kossuth led Hungarian Revolution reunited Transylvania with

Hungary. The union was dissolved after the revolution was crushed, but revived after the 1867 Dual Monarchy came into being. Transylvania remained part of Hungary until World War I ended with the military defeat of the Dual Monarchy.

In this 1,000 years of history the demographic profile of Hungary and Transylvania underwent a drastic change. Most of the change came after the Turkish and Habsburg conquests. The Hungarian Kingdom had been multi-ethnic from the very beginning. Together with the Hungarians the land was also inhabited by Slovaks, Slovenes, Germans, Croats, Serbs, Petchenegs, Cumans, Jazigs, Vlachs (Romanians), and Bulgars. However, as late as 1490 under Matthias Rex (Hunyadi) the four million inhabitants of the Carpathian Basin were still predominantly Hungarian (approximately 80%) in language and culture. The devastating Turkish wars and occupation reduced the total population of the Kingdom by the end of the 17th century to less than two million. Of this two million only about 45 percent were still Hungarians. Habsburg policy attempted to consolidate its power by encouraging other peoples to settle in the depopulated Hungarian territories. It is in the context of these last four centuries that Transylvania acquired a Romanian majority while the other peoples, Swabian-Germans, Saxon-Germans, Serbs, and Hungarians came to compose less than 45 percent of the region's population. Changes in the sovereignty over Transylvania simply reinforced the demographic advantages of the Romanians. The present chronology will pick up the train of developments from World War I which led to the collapse of the Austro-Hungarian Monarchy and the annexation of Transylvania by Romania.

1914 July 28. Beginning of World War I
1916 August 17. The Entente promises Transylvania to Romania if she enters the war on their side.
1918 October 27. Austria-Hungary pushes for an armistice.
1918 November 12-14. Oszkár Jászi negotiates with Iuliu Maniu in Arad. The Romanian leaders reject the Hungarian offer of autonomy within Transylvania and instead demand independence.
1918 December 1-2. The Romanian assembly convoked in Alba Iulia (Gyulafehérvár) declares union of Transylvania with the Kingdom of Romania. (The document also promises equality to non-Romanians and their right to national cultural autonomy).
1918 December 2. Romanian military occupation begins in Transylvania.

1919 January 11. The Romanian government proclaims the annexation of Transylvania.
1919 March 20. The Allies' "Vix Ultimatum" orders Hungary to withdraw from territories to be occupied by Romania. President Mihály Károlyi and the Hungarian government resign in protest.
1919 March 21. Béla Kun's communist dictatorship comes to power in Budapest.
1919 April. Romanian and Czech armies attack Béla Kun's Hungarian Soviet Republic. While the Czech armies are pushed back, the Romanian armies continue their advance.
1919 August 1. Fall of Béla Kun's Soviet Republic and the subsequent restoration of the Hungarian Kingdom with Admiral Miklós Horthy as Regent.
1920 June 4. The Peace Treaty of Trianon partitions historic Hungary and assigns Romania an area of 102,000 sq. km. with a total population of 3.5 million of which 1,664,000 are Hungarians according to the census of 1910.
1920 August 14-June 7, 1921. The Little Entente comes into being to defend the newly acquired territories of Czechoslovakia, Yugoslavia, and Romania against Hungarian revisionism.
1921 June 5. Károly Kós and others establish the Hungarian People's Party in Huedin (Bánffyhunyad).
1922 February 12. Founding of the Hungarian National Party which then merges with the Hungarian People's Party on December 28th of that year and becomes the National Hungarian Party. The latter publishes the political review *Magyar Kisebbség* (Hungarian Minority) for the next twenty years under the editorship of Elemér Jakabffy in Lugoj (Lugos).
1923 March 29. The new Romanian Constitution is adopted. It guarantees general equality to all but does not include any of the minority rights guaranteed in the peace treaties or the promises of the 1918 Alba Iulia declarations.
1924 June 26. The Romanian Primary Education Act provides special benefits to Romanian teachers in national minority areas to counteract "denationalization by alien elements."
1925. The law on private education demands that geography, history, and the constitution of Romania be taught in Romanian. The teaching of the Romanian language also becomes compulsory in all

schools and all school teachers must pass Romanian language examinations.
1927 April 5. To break out of its isolation by the Little Entente, Hungary signs a treaty of friendship and cooperation with Italy.
1927 April 22. The statute regulating religious practice deprives the minority churches of their autonomy and puts them under the supervision of the central government.
1930. According to the Romanian census 1,425,507 people claimed Hungarian nationality and 1,554,525 people claimed Hungarian as their mother tongue.
1933. Hitler's rise to power in Germany throws the question of border revision into the center of European politics.
1933. Construction of the Romanian Orthodox Cathedral in Cluj (Kolozsvár).
1934 August. The left wing of the Hungarian Party in Romania reconstitutes itself as the National Union of Hungarian Workers (MADOSZ).
1935 December 6. MADOSZ joins the Antifascist Democratic Front.
1936. Hungarian industrial corporations are dissolved by a new trade law and their property is assigned to the Romanian state-managed chamber of industry.
1936-46. Construction of Romanian Orthodox Cathedral in Timisoara (Temesvár).
1938. King Carol II declares a royal dictatorship in Romania and disbands all political parties.
1938 August 14. Romania's Public Administration Act divides the country into ten provinces in such a way that Romanians gain an ethnic predominance in each of the new subdivisions.
1938 November 2. Czechoslovakia's Hungarian inhabited territories are returned to Hungary by the Axis arbitrated First Vienna Award. This raises Hungarian hopes for possible territorial revision in relation to Transylvania.
1939 August 23. Nazi-Soviet Non-Aggression Pact is signed.
1939 September 1. Hitler invades Poland beginning World War II.
1940 June. Romania cedes Bessarabia and northern Bukovina to the USSR.
1940 August 16-23. Romanian-Hungarian negotiations for frontier rectification breaks down.

1940 August 30. Through Axis arbitration the Second Vienna Award returns northern Transylvania to Hungary. It included most of the Hungarian-inhabited regions, but it still leaves about half a million Hungarians in Romania. About 200,000 Romanians leave Hungary and 60,000 Hungarians leave Romania across the newly established border.
1941 June 22. Romania joins the Nazi attack on the Soviet Union.
1941 June 27. Hungary enters the war against the USSR.
1944 March 19. Hungary is occupied by Germany.
1944 August 23. Romania swiches sides in the war, sues for an armistice and declares war on Germany on August 25th.
1944 September 12. Armistice signed between Romania and USSR. The latter promises Transylvania "or the greater part thereof" to Romania for its abandonment of the Axis war effort.
1944 October. Romanian administration is restored in the reconquered areas of northern Transylvania. However, massacres perpetrated by the Maniu Guardists against Hungarians leads to the establishment of Soviet administration over the region to forestall further atrocities.
1945 February 4-12. The Yalta Conference provides for the consolidation of Soviet control over both Romania and Hungary.
1945 March 6. Communists come to power in Romania under the leadership of Petru Groza and Gheorghiu-Dej pledging the protection of minorities. Three days later the USSR grants the restoration of Romanian administration over northern Transylvania.
1945 March 23. Land reform decree dramatically reduces the economic opportunities of 300,000 Hungarian small-holders in Transylvania.
1945 March 30. The Citizenship Act leaves 200,000 Hungarians without rights. Thousands are forced to emigrate.
1945 April 2. Decree on minority languages makes their use "legal" and in the postal service and on the railroads bilingual signs become obligatory.
1945 May 29. The Bolyai State University is organized in Cluj (Kolozsvár), thereby reestablishing Hungarian university level education in Transylvania.
1946. A general revival of Hungarian cultural opportunities takes place as the Hungarian People's Union increases Hungarian representation in the Romanian parliament and as primary and sec-

ondary schools again begin to function. Two additional important examples are the opening of the Székely State Theater of Tîrgu Mureş (Marosvásárhely) and the publication of the literary weekly *Utunk* (Our Way) under the editorship of Gábor Gaál.

1946 July 17 - August 2. The Potsdam Conference reaffirms the pledges of the Yalta agreements.

1947 February 10. Hungary signs the Peace Treaty of Paris concluding World War II. It reaffirms the pre-1938 Trianon boundaries and assigns two Hungarian bridgeheads near Bratislava to Slovakia.

1947 August. The Csángó-Hungarians receive their first Hungarian language schools. (These are later eliminated in the 1950s).

1947 December 30. King Michael of Romania abdicates under Soviet pressure. The Communists consolidate their hold over the country.

1948 January. The official Romanian census claims that there are 1,499,851 Hungarians in the country. This is 9.4 percent of the population.

1948 March 6. The People's Democratic (Communist) Constitution is adopted.

1948. Stalin expels Tito's Yugoslavia from the Cominform.

1948 August 3. Private education, and church schools are eliminated by the new educational law. At the same time it establishes seven-year compulsory education.

1948 September. The Hungarian Opera is reestablished in Cluj (Kolozsvár).

1949 January 25. Soviet control is tightened over the Soviet Bloc via the organization of economic integration through COMECON.

1949 June 21. The Hungarian Roman Catholic Bishop of Alba Iulia (Gyulafehérvár). Áron Márton is imprisoned. He is released in 1955 but kept under house arrest until 1967.

1949 October. Most of the leaders of the Hungarian People's Union are accused of treason and imprisoned. Many are released in 1955, but the organization's president (Gyárfás Kurkó) is released only in 1965.

1952. The "minority" representatives, Ana Pauker and Vasile Luka are purged from the top leadership of the Romanian Workers' Party.

1952 September 24. Romania adopts a new Constitution which also parallels the establishment of a Hungarian Autonomous Region in eastern Transylvania, granting some measure of symbolic self-government to the solidly Hungarian Székely population.
1953 March 5. Stalin dies.
1953. The Hungarian People's Union is disbanded.
1955 May 11-15. The Warsaw Pact tightens Moscow's control over the bloc by integrating its military forces in a Soviet led military alliance.
1956 February. Nikita S. Khrushchev denounces Stalin at the 20th Party Congress of the CPSU.
1956 October. Unrest breaks out in Poland and spreads to Hungary. On October 23 this erupts into a national revolution against the USSR and its Hungarian lackeys. The events there trigger sympathy demonstrations throughout Transylvania in Hungarian inhabited cities like Cluj (Kolozsvár), Oradea (Nagyvárad), Timişoara (Temesvár), and Tîrgu Mureş (Marosvásárhely). Throughout Romania this is followed by the mass arrest, deportation and imprisonment of Hungarians.
1956 November 4. Soviet military intervention, with Czech and Romanian logistic support, crushes the Hungarian Revolution and installs the János Kádár regime.
1957. Purge of Miron Constantinescu and Iosif Chisinevschi by Gheorghe Gheorghiu-Dej consolidates the ethnic Romanian cadres in the top leadership positions.
1957. The periodical *Korunk* (Our Age) resumes publication in Cluj (Kolozsvár).
1958. Soviet troops are withdrawn from Romania as a reward for the country's loyalty during the Hungarian Revolution. This is paralleled by a new wave of minority oppression.
1959 February 22. The Hungarian Bolyai University of Cluj (Kolozsvár) is merged with the Romanian Babeş University and renamed Babeş-Bolyai University. At all lower levels of education as well a similar merger leads to the absorption of Hungarian schools by Romanian schools.
1960 December 24. The Hungarian Autonomous Region is gerrymandered and renamed the Mureş-Maghiar Autonomous Region. The Hungarian portion of the population is thereby diluted to 62 percent from 77.3 percent of the total.

1962 April. The collectivization of agriculture is completed with particularly discriminatory consequences for the Hungarian rural population in Transylvania.
1964. Romania begins to assert its independence from COMECON in determining its economic policy options within the Socialist bloc.
1965 March 22. Soon after the death of Gheorghiu-Dej, Nicolae Ceausescu is elected First Secretary of the Central Committee of the Romanian Communist Party.
1965 August 21. A new constitution is adopted by Romania which redefines it as a Socialist Republic.
1966. The official census claims that 1,619,592 persons defined themselves as Hungarians by nationality while 1,653,873 claimed Hungarian as their mother tongue.
1968 February 16. Romania's Grand National Assembly uses the territorial reorganization of the country as a pretext to eliminate the Mureş-Maghiar Autonomous Region.
1968 August 20. The "Brezhnev doctrine" is used by the USSR to justify its invasion of Czechoslovakia with its Warsaw Pact allies. Romania refuses to support this action, fearing similar intervention in its own domestic affairs.
1968 November 15. To establish a united front against possible external intervention, the Ceausescu regime begins to make some concessions to minority concerns. As a first step Council of Workers of Hungarian Nationality is established. However, this is merely a symbolic organization with no legal status to represent the Hungarian nationality in Romanian policy-making.
1969 September. The University of Bucharest re-opens a department of Hungarian literature and philology.
1969 November. A series of cultural concessions are made to the Hungarian minority, including some limited broadcasts in Hungarian on Romanian television and the establishment of the non-Romanian nationalities publishing house, Kriterion.
1970 October. A new Hungarian-language weekly, *A Hét* (The Week) begins publication in Bucharest.
1971 June. For the first time a leader of the Hungarian Socialist Workers' Party, Zoltán Komocsin, publicly declares that Hungary is interested in the fate of the Hungarian national minority in Romania.

1973 May 19. Educational decree law 271 is published. It narrows the educational opportunity of the Hungarian minority even further, particularly in small rural communities, by requiring a minimum number of students per class. No such minimum number is established for Romanians even in areas inhabited mainly by minorities.

1974. A decree reduces the size of newspapers and the number of pages and issues per publication. Ostensibly this is an emergency measure in the face of a paper shortage. In actuality it hits the minority press hardest, dealing a crippling blow to some of the best Hungarian-language periodicals and newspapers.

1974 November. A law is promulgated to defend Romania's cultural heritage, which makes all archival materials "the property of the people." In this way all minority church (Catholic, Lutheran, Calvinist, etc.) documents are subject to confiscation and collection by the central authorities. This reflects the state's aggressive desire to obliterate the history of minorities while at the same time it Romanianizes the history of Transylvania.

1975. A decree goes into effect which requires all foreign visitors to stay in hotels during their sojourn in Romania. Its purpose is to reduce contact between Transylvanian Hungarians and their relatives and friends from neighboring countries.

1975 July 30-August 1. The Final Act of the Helsinki Conference on Security and Cooperation in Europe includes in "Basket III" the affirmation of the rights of minorities.

1975. President Gerald Ford of the USA grants Romania MFN (Most Favored Nation) status.

1976. Establishment of CHRR (The Committee for Human Rights in Romania) in New York City under the leadership of László Hámos and others to monitor the violations of the Helsinki Accord in relation to the Hungarian and other minorities in Romania.

1977 June 15-16. János Kádár meets with Nicolae Ceausescu in Debrecen (Hungary) and Oradea (Romania) to try and reconcile some of their differences. The meeting pays lipservice to "building bridges" but does not lead to the betterment of inter-ethnic relations in Romania.

1978. Károly Király, a prominent Hungarian member of the Romanian Communist Party sent protest letters to his leadership concerning the oppression of the Hungarian minority. From CHRR the Western press obtains copies of these protests. The Romanian authorities force Király into internal exile and attempt to isolate him from contact with the outside world.

1978. The first Helsinki review conference meets in Belgrade to discuss the human rights performance of the signatory states. The Károly Király letters are circulated at this conference.

1981 December. Hungarian intellectuals in Transylvania launch an underground periodical, *Ellenpontok* (Counterpoints) against the minority oppression of the Ceausescu regime.

1982 September. The editors of *Ellenpontok* submit a memorandum to the Madrid conference reviewing adherence to the Helsinki Final Act. It calls for the creation of an international commission to investigate the situation in Transylvania.

1982. The publication of a number of anti-Hungarian hate works (including Ion Lancranjan's *A Word about Transylvania*) incites the Romanians against the country's largest minority.

1983. The Madrid conference reviewing compliance with the Helsinki Final Act, in its closing document reiterates the rights of national minorities.

1983 May. Romania expels Attila Ara-Kovács for his part in the submission of the memorandum to the Madrid conference.

1984 July. Romania expels Károly Tóth for his role in relation to the Madrid memorandum.

1985 September. Géza Szőcs submits a petition to the Central Committee of the Romanian Communist party demanding the release of all political prisioners, including Ernő Borbély and László Balázs.

1986 August. Romania expels Géza Szőcs.

1986 November. At the third Helsinki review conference in Vienna, the Hungarian delegate László Demus indicates that Hungary is very much concerned about the fate of Hungarians living in neighboring states and condemns nationalism and forced assimilation.

1987 May 26. During his official visit to Bucharest, Soviet leader Mikhail S. Gorbachev chides the Romanians on excercising more care and sensitivity in the treatment of their minority nationalities.

1987. After defecting from Romania, Ceausescu's former spy chief, Ion Mihai Pacepa, writes *Red Horizons* which reveals the corrup-

tion, brutality and oppressive policies of the Romanian establishment.
1987. The U.S. Congress votes to revoke Romania's MFN status in large measure because of its dismal record in human rights violations and abuse of minorities.
1988 April. Ceausescu's administration publicizes a "bulldozing" plan to eliminate 7,000 villages before the end of the century. The objective is to establish new agro-industrial centers where the various national groups would be absorbed by the majority Romanian population.
1989 November. At the Party Congress of the Romanian Communist Party, Ceausescu still holds the line against any form of revisionism.
1989 December 18. In Timişoara (Temesvár) the attempt by the Romanian *Securitate* (security police) to evict Rev. László Tőkés from his Hungarian Reformed church, leads to a mass demonstration against the Ceausescu regime. The demonstration is attacked by the *Securitate*. Instead of dispersing, the demonstrators fight back. The unrest spreads to other cities, including Bucharest.
1989 December 22. Ceausescu flies back from a state visit to Iran only to find that his political support at home is evaporating. He flees the capital by helicopter but is captured and returned to Bucharest.
1989 December 25. After a kangaroo trial by his former supporters, Nicolae and Elena Ceausescu are executed by a firing squad in Bucharest.

Endnotes

1. To understand the historical roots of Transylvania and the ethnic conflict in that region, see Hugh Seton-Watson, *Nations and States: An Inquiry into the Origins of Nations and the Politics of Nationalism* (London, 1977), pp. 157-169, 175-185; Elemér Mélyusz, ed., *Siebenbürgen and seine Völkerschaften* (Budapest-Leipzig, 1943); Constantin C. Giurescu and Dinu C. Giurescu, *Geschichte der Rumänen* (Bucharest, 1980); Constantin C. Giurescu, *Transylvania in the History of Romania* (London, n.d. c. 1970); John F. Cadzow, Andrew Ludanyi and Louis Elteto eds., *Transylvania: Roots of Ethnic Conflict* (Kent, Ohio, 1983); Miron Constantinescu and Stefan Pascu, *Unification of the Romanian National State* (Bucharest, 1971); Ceausescu, Ilie, *Transylvanie, terre ancienne roumaine* (Bucharest, 1984); Király, Pastor, Sanders eds., *Essays on the World War I: Total War and Peacemaking, A Case Study on Trianon.* (New York, 1982); Stephen Borsody ed., *The Hungarians: A Divided Nation* (New Haven, 1988); Stephen Fischer-Galati, *Twentieth Century Rumania,* (New York, 1979); Elemér Illyés, *National Minorities in Romania: Change in Transylvania* (New York, 1982) esp. pp. 9-28.

2. Béla Köpeczi, ed., *Erdély története* [History of Transylvania] 3 vols. (Budapest, 1986).

3. The estimated figures provided in parentheses are more reliable and provide a more accurate picture of the current strength of the minority population.

4. Borsody, *Hungarians,* XXI-XXVIII, 3-31.

5. György Schöpflin, "Az emberi jogok és a nemzetiségi kérdés Romániában" [Human rights and the nationality question in Romania], *Századvég* (1987) pp. 108-120; "The Ideology of Rumanian Nationalism," *Survey* 20, Nos. 2-3: 77-104.

6. *Recensămintul populatiei si al locuintelor din 5 ianuarie 1977* (Bucharest, 1977), 1, pp. 614-621.

7. See A. Golopentia and D.C. Georgescu, *Populatia Republicii Populare Romanei la 25 ianuarie 1948 (Probleme Economice 1948 martie)* pp. 28-45; *Recensamintul populaiiei din 21 februarie 1956 Recensamintul populatiei si locuintelor din 15 martie 1966 Recensamintul populatiei si al locuintelor din 5 ianuarie 1977.* I. 614-621.

8. George Schöpflin, *The Hungarians of Rumania* (London, 1978) p. 6; Illyés, *National Minorities,* p. 33; Zoltán Dávid, "Magyarok – határaink mentén" [Hungarians along Our borders], *Mozgó Világ,* 1982: 7, pp. 38-50.

9. See Illyés, *National Minorities,* pp. 11-12; Gergely Csoma and Pál Péter Domokos, *Moldvai csángó magyarok* [The Csángó Hungarians of Moldavia] (Budapest, 1988).

10. Schöpflin, *Hungarians of Rumania,* p. 6; Illyés, *National Minorities,* pp. 31-33.

11. Reports of the Hungarian Press of Transylvania (HPT); *Rumänien und die Menschenrechte anliegen der Minderheiten* (Zürich, 1987) pp. 6-7.

12. For the official presentation of the "systematization project" see Zoltán Mihálka," Területrendezés – átfogó és komplex program az ország helységeinek felvirágoztatására" [Systematization – a global and complex program in order to bring prosperity to the settlements of the country], *Előre,* June 14, 1988. Among foreign reactions, see "A magyar Országgyűlés állásfoglalása a romániai 'területrendezési' programról" [The statement of the Hungarian Parliament on the "settlement systematization project" in Romania], *Magyar Nemzet,* July 2, 1988; "Resolution on new measures liquidating villages in Romania." Text adopted by the *European Parliament,* Thursday, July 7, 1988; *U.S. Senate* Resolution 461 condemning Romania for its human rights violations. August 11, 1988; Resolution of the Executive Committee of the *Federal Union of European Nationalities (FUEN)* Antwerp, September 16-17, 1988; in *Erdély-Siebenbürgen-Transylvania (*Felsőör-Oberwart, 1988), p.

19; Janet Heller, "Ceausescu, Cultural Vandal," *The New York Times,* December 12, 1988.

13. See Illyés, *National Minorities,* pp. 66-67; Schöpflin, *Hungarians of Rumania,* pp. 13-14; Transylvanian World Federation, *Rumania's Violations of the Helsinki Final Act Provisions* (Berlin, 1980), pp. 40-42.

14. Björn Cato Funnemark, *S.O.S. Transylvania* (Vienna, 1988), pp. 38-39.

15. Hungarian Press of Transylvania, December 1988.

16. See e.g., some statutes concerning the minorities, in "Documents".

17. See "Documents" at the end of the study.

18. *Ibid.*

19. For more details, see Illyés, *National Minorities,* pp. 94-111; and Köpeczi, ed., *Erdély története,* vol. 3, 1759-1762; György Beke, "Nemzetiségi létfeltételek építése Erdélyben 1944 és 1948 között" [The evolution of the status of minorities in Transylvania between 1944 and 1948], *Forrás,* 1982: 8, pp. 80-86.

20. *Világosság,* 1946: 7, 7.

21. Ildikó Lipcsey, "A romániai Népi Szövetség 1944-48" [The Hungarian People's Federation in Romania, 1944-48], *Történelmi Szemle,* 1985/1, pp. 96-117.

22. The original text of the two previous constitutions can be found in *Monitorul Oficial,* I, no. 87/1948, April 13, 1948; *Buletinul Oficial* no. 1, 1952. The revised text of the 1965 constitution is in *Buletinul Oficial* no. 56, 1974.

23. For an excellent discussion of the "gerrymandering" policy of the Romanian government toward the Hungarian Autonomous Region, see Walker Connor, *The National Question in Marxist-Leninist Theory and Strategy* (Princeton, 1984), pp. 237-238, 340-342.

24. *Buletinul Oficial* no. 56/1974.

25. *Ibid.*

26. *Buletinul Oficial I*, no. 113/1978, December 26, 1978.
27. Schöpflin, *The Hungarians of Rumania*, p. 9.
28. A detailed presentation of these developments is given in Sándor Koppándi, ed., *A romániai magyar nemzetiség* [The Hungarian nationality in Romania], (Bucuresti, 1981).
29. For the text of the law-decree, see "Documents".
30. *Ibid.*
31. *Ibid.*
32. *Ibid.*
33. For details on the Romanian historic evolution on this matter see George Schöpflin, "The Ideology of Romanian Nationalism," *Survey*, 20/2-3, pp. 77-104. From the same author, "Transylvania: Hungarians under Romanian Rule," in Borsody, ed., *The Hungarians: A Divided Nation*, pp. 119-158.
34. Illyés, *National Minorities*, p. 137.
35. See, e.g., the statements made at the joint session of Councils of Hungarian and German Nationality Workers. *Igazság*, March 4, 1987; *Előre*, March 1-5, 1987.
36. Based on interviews with Transylvanian refugees in Hungary.
37. See Károly Király's letters in *Witnesses to Cultural Genocide: Firsthand Reports on Rumania's Minority Policies* (New York, 1979), pp. 162-178.
38. About the general human rights abuses and the "minority policy" pursued by the *Securitate* and the Romanian party-state as a whole see Ion Mihai Pacepa, *Red Horizons: Chronicles of a Communist Spy Chief,* (Washington D.C., 1987).
39. The Iron Guard, an extreme right-wing organization, supported Hitler and his policies during World War II. It was responsible for stirring up numerous anti-Semitic and anti-Hungarian activities, including the instigation of riots in Braşov (Brassó), Aiud (Nagyenyed), and Cluj (Kolozsvár) in 1936.

40. The Daco-Roman continuity theory and its place in the Romanian-Hungarian conflict receives extensive treatment in Hugh Seton-Watson, *Nations and States* (Boulder, 1977), pp. 175-185; Andrew Ludányi, "Ideology and Political Culture in Rumania: The Daco-Roman Theory and the 'Place' of Minorities," in Cadzow, Ludanyi, Elteto, eds., *Transylvania: The Roots of Ethnic Conflict,* pp. 229-244.

41. Some examples of incitement of hatred against Hungarians and of the deliberate falsification of history are Ion Lancranjan, *The Story of Transylvania* (Bucharest, 1982); Ion Lancranjan, *Toamna fierbinte* [Hot Autumn] (Bucharest, 1986); *Teroarea Horthysto-fascista in Nordvestul Romaniei, septembrie 1940-octobrie 1944.* [Horthyite fascist terror in northwest Romania, September 1940 to October 1944] (Bucharest, 1985). Also see the accounts of the meetings of the Councils of Hungarian and German Nationality Workers in *Előre,* March 1-5, 1987, and *Igazság,* March 4, 1987.

42. Based on personal interviews with refugees from Transylvania.

43. For an analyses of the literary expression of the minority grievances, see Károly Nagy, *"Patterns of Minority Life: Recent Hungarian Literary Reports in Romania,"* in *Society in Change: Studies in Honor of Béla K. Király,* Steven Bela Vardy and Agnes Huszár Vardy, eds., New York, 1983), pp. 585-595. For the opposition of some Catholic and Protestant priests to the religious and minority persecution, see Funnemark, *S.O.S. Transylvania,* p. 52. For a presentation of protest-suicide cases, see Robert R. King, *Minorities Under Communism* (Cambridge, 1973), p. 154.

44. For a collection of minority representatives' letters, memoranda and situation reports, see *Witnesses in Cultural Genocide; Rumänien und die Menschenrechte,* Anhang, 2/A-2/D.

45. See "Documents."

46. Koppándi, ed., *A romániai magyar nemzetiség,* pp. 449-461.

47. Illyés, *National Minorities,* pp. 248-249.

48. See footnote 35 and *Előre,* 1978: 2, 28; *Korunk,* 1978: 3.

49. *Erdély története,* Vol. 3, 1773-1774; Beke, "Nemzetiségi létfeltételek ...," pp. 80-86.

50. For the connections of this development with the 1956 revolution in Hungary, see also, Andrew Ludanyi, "The Revolution and the Fate of Hungarians in Neighboring States," in Király, Lotze, Dreisziger, eds., *The First War Between Socialist States: The Hungarian Revolution of 1956 and its Impact* (New York, 1984), pp. 393-397; King, *Minorities,* pp. 152-153.

51. *Buletinul Oficial,* no. 6 1969.

52. Based on personal interviews with refugees from Transylvania.

53. Attila Ara-Kovács, *A nyolcvanas évek Romániája és az erdélyi magyarság* [Romania in the Eighties and the Hungarians of Transylvania], Manuscript, Budapest, 1987, and *Reports of the Hungarian Press of Transylvania.*

54. These official figures were used in *A Living Reality in Romania Today: Full Harmony and Equality Between the Romanian People and the Coinhabiting Nationalities* (n.p., n.d.).

55. Institute for Hungarian Studies *A Romániában élő magyarok helyzetéről* [On the Situation of Hungarians Living in Romania], Manuscript, Budapest, 1987. See "Documents."

56. Based on interview with the person now living in Hungary.

57. See the declaration by the Hungarian Writers Association, "Szolidaritás Kányádi Sándorral" [Solidarity with Sándor Kányádi], *Élet és Irodalom,* 1987: 10.

58. See *Witnesses to Cultural Genocide,* pp. 145-161.

59. Institute for Hungarian Studies *A Romániában élő magyarok helyzetéről,* p. 17.

60. See footnote 58.

61. This process began already in 1974. For details, see Schöpflin, *The Hungarians in Rumania,* p. 13.

62. For further details, see Lajos Für, "Hungarian History as Taught by Hungary's Neighbors," in Borsody, ed., *The Hungarians: A Divided Nation*, pp. 303-307.

63. "Az erdélyi magyar és szász kultúra veszélyeztetett emlékei" [The threatened monuments of the Hungarian and Saxon Cultures in Transylvania]. A list provided by the Hungarian Press of Transylvania. Cluj (Kolozsvár), April 1987, Manuscript, p. 4.

64. For a general introduction to Hungarian theatrical life, see the corresponding chapter of Koppándi, ed., *A romániai magyar nemzetiség*, pp. 462-477.

65. Institute for Hungarian Studies *A Romániában élő magyarok helyzetéről* p. 16.

66. Funnemark, *S.O.S. Transylvania*, p. 42.

67. See the testimony concerning the harassment of the collectors in Moldavia in "Les Hongrois de Transylvanie," *Esprit*, 1978: 3, pp. 64-84.

68. See, Helsinki Watch, *Human Rights in Rumania* (New York, 1984), pp. 17-29; Sergiu Grossu, *Le Calvaire de la Roumanie chrétienne* (Paris, 1987); Janice Broun, "Religion in Romania: The Truth Behind the Image," *Freedom at Issue*, March-April, 1984.

69. Grossu, *Le Calvaire*, p. 199.

70. *Ibid.*

71. *Ibid.* For examples, see Mircea Pacurariu's and Antonie Plamandeala's books in the "Bibliographie."

72. Illyés, *National Minorities*, p. 220.

73. *Református egyház a Román Szocialista Köztársaságban* [The Calvinist Church in the Socialist Republic of Rumania], (Cluj-Kolozsvár, 1961).

74. E.g., see Funnemark, *S.O.S. Transylvania*, p. 48.

75. *Buletinul Oficial*, no. 56 1974.

76. A detailed elaboration of the subject can be found in Illyés, *National Minorities*, pp. 218-237; Funnemark, *S.O.S. Transylvania*, pp. 45-48; Schöpflin, *The Hungarians in Rumania*, pp. 7-8. For the presentation of recent developments we mainly used the written or oral communications of clergymen living in Hungary or Romania; the minutes of the debate over the extension of the MFN status to Romania is published in, *Congressional Record, Senate,* Washington, June 26, 1987; *Congressional Record, House,* Washington, February 18, 1988.

77. *Ibid.*

78. *Ibid.*

79. See Matatias Carp, *Cartea neagre despre suferintele evreilor din Romania* [Black book on the suffering of the Jews of Romania], (Bucharest, 1947); I.C. Butnaru, *Holocaustul uitat* [The forgotten Holocaust] (Tel Aviv, 1985).

80. On this phenomenon, see King, *Minorities Under Communism,* p. 148. Committee for Human Rights in Rumania, "Minority Oppression in Rumania: A One Year Record, May 1983-June 1984." (New York, 1984), pp. 26-30.

81. *Country Reports on Human Rights Practices for 1985,* Washington, February, 1986, p. 1084.

82. Based on personal interviews with refugees from Transylvania.

83. The fact is also confirmed by *Country Reports,* p. 1084.

84. Helsinki Watch, *Human Rights in Rumania,* p. 48; Schöpflin, *The Hungarians of Rumania,* p. 15.

85. *Ibid.*

86. On the limitation of personal contacts, see Helsinki Watch *Human Rights in Rumania,* p. 49.

87. See footnote 83.

88. Based on communications delivered by the organizers of the three conferences.

89. See also, Schöpflin, *The Hungarians of Rumania,* p. 15.

90. *Le Monde,* April 9, 1988, p. 7; *Magyar Hírlap,* April 6, 1988, p. 3.

91. Rudolf Joó, "Kisebbségek a nemzetközi kapcsolatokban" [Minorities in international relations], *Századvég,* 1987: 4-5, p. 105.

92. See also, Pierre Kende, "Communist Hungary and the Hungarian Minorities," in Borsody, ed., *The Hungarians,* pp. 280-281.

93. *Ibid.,* pp. 274-276.

94. From Károly Vigh's lecture, delivered at the Hungarian Democratic Forum's meeting held in Budapest on March 6, 1988, dealing with minorities beyond the Hungarian borders.

95. Lajos Für, "Nemzetiségi kérdés – nemzetiségtudományi kutatások" [Ethnic problems – ethnic studies], *Valóság,* 1982: 1, pp. 34-46.

96. See the joint statements issued after top level diplomatic talks between Hungary and neighboring states in *Népszabadság,* April 30, 1974; *Népszabadság,* February 3, 1977; *Népszabadság,* April 28, 1976; *Népszabadság,* June 17, 1977.

97. This concern and criticism was expressed in a letter from 19 Hungarian intellectuals to the First Secretary of the HSWP Central Committee on the matter of Hungarian minorities, dated July 27, 1984.

98. For the changing pattern of the Hungarian policy in this matter, see also, Bennett Kovrig, "The Magyars in Romania: Problems of a 'Cohabiting' Nationality," *Südosteuropa,* 35 (1986) h.9, pp. 475-490.

99. See *Magyar Hírlap,* January 27, 1988.

100. Imre Szokai - Csaba Tabajdi, "Mai politikánk és a nemzetiségi kérdés" [Our policy today and the nationality question], *Magyar Nemzet,* February 13, 1988.

101. Illyés, *National Minorities,* p. 23.

102. *Ibid.,* p. 24.

103. For the text, see United Nations, *Droits de l'Homme. Recueil d'instruments internationaux*, (New York, 1983), p. 10.
104. Amnesty International, *1987 Report*, (London, 1987), p. 310.
105. *Ibid.*, pp. 309-311.
106. Figures provided by the Hungarian Press of Transylvania.
107. Pacepa, *Red Horizons,* p. 73, quotes Ceausescu saying, "We've also got to up the price Tel Aviv and Bonn are paying for Jews and Germans. ... Oil, Jews, and Germans are our most important export commodities!"
108. For the demographic change of this group in the post-war period, see Table I, p. 29 above.
109. On the negative consequences of the mass emigration for the survival of the German community in Transylvania, see e.g., a Transylvanian bishop's opinion in "Siebenbürgens Bischof bestürzt über Bonner Freikauf-Pläne," *Süddeutsche Zeitung,* August 9, 1988.
110. Pacepa, *Red Horizons,* p. 75, contends that the going price was even higher. He states, "The new ...agreement provided that Bucharest would be paid, in cash, a certain amount per head, depending on age, education, profession, employment, and family status, for each Jew allowed to emigrate. In July 1978, this payment amounted to between $2,000 and $50,000 per person. In some individual cases ...up to $250,000."
111. Géza Szőcs then left Romania to find asylum in in the West. After Ceausescu's overthrow he repatriated and is now Senator in the Romanian Parliament.
112. *Magyar Hírlap,* January 29, 1988.
113. *Ibid.*
114. Based on the personal accounts of refugees involved in the matter.
115. A list of Hungarian religious charitable organizations dealing with refugees is provided in the booklet *10 kérdés az erdélyi*

menekültekről [10 Questions on the Transylvanian Refugees] (Budapest, 1988), pp. 54-55.

116. Appeal of the Asylum Committee. Made public in Budapest, January 29, 1988.

117. The functions of the "Interdepartmental Committee" were presented in an interview with its secretary in *10 kérdés az erdélyi menekültekről*, pp. 24-27.

118. See, e.g., the statement and recommendations of the Hungarian Democratic Forum concerning the Hungarian minority in Romania and Transylvanian refugees, March 6, 1988.

Documents

A

Statute on Opening of Classes Taught in the Languages of the Nationalities and in Romanian

Law-Decree No. 273/1973 of the State Council

on the establishment of uniform rules of organization in educational institutions.

The State Council of the Socialist Republic of Romania decrees:

(...)

II. Compulsory primary education

Compulsory primary education is delivered through primary schools controlled by the people's councils.

Primary schools shall be organized as follows:
- Schools with grades 1-8 are to be opened in localities where the number of students to be enrolled in grade 5 is at least 25;
- Schools with grades 1-10 are to be opened in localities where the number of students to be enrolled in grade 9 is at least 25.

In isolated localities where primary schools with 8 or 10 grades cannot be organized, schools with grades 1-4 shall be organized if there are at least 7 children of an age appropriate to these classes.

In those communities with schools teaching in the languages of cohabiting nationalities, sections or classes taught in Rumanian shall be organized, irrespective of the number of students.

Dormitories, day-care centers, or canteens associated with the primary schools may be organized for at least 50 students. In justified cases (isolated localities with few children, long distances, or other special circumstances), the Ministry of Public Education may sanction the establishment of dormitories, day-care centres, or canteens for less than the above required number of students.

III. Secondary education and technical-vocational training

Secondary education and technical-vocational training are provided by general secondary schools, vocational schools, trade schools, and post-secondary schools which, depending on the circumstances, are controlled by the people's councils, the ministries, other central organs or industrial centres, and which may function independently or within a school complex comprising at least two educational establishments.

Secondary school and technical-vocational training establishments may be organized with at least two classes in the first year of their operation.

The number of students per class shall be 36 on the average. The Ministry of Public Education may exceptionally consent to the operation of certain classes with at least 25 students each in the last two school years.

In secondary schools with instruction in the language of cohabiting nationalities, sections or classes taught in Romanian shall be organized, irrespective of the number of students.

In the interest of providing necessary conditions of board and lodging, dormitories and daycare centers with canteens may be organized for at least 100 students. In well justified cases, the Ministry of Public Education may sanction the maintenance of certain residence halls, daycare centres or canteens for less than the required number of students.

Bucharest, May 13, 1973

(signed) Nicolae Ceausescu
President
of the Socialist Republic of Romania

(*Source: Monitorul Oficial,* Vol. IX. No. 67. Part I. May 13, 1973)

B

Statute on the Accomodation of Foreign Citizens

Law-Decree No. 225/1974 of the State Council

on the provision of lodging for foreigners temporarily staying in Romania.

The State Council of the Socialist Republic of Romania decrees:

Art. 1. In order to provide foreigners temporarily staying in Romania as tourists or for any other purpose with the most appropriate housing conditions possible, the persons concerned shall be accomodated in hotels, motels, campsites and hostels, as well as in any other lodgings belonging to the dwelling fund administered by socialist organizations.

Lodgings differing in function from the apartments required by foreigners temporarily residing in Romania or by foreign juristic persons shall be allocated out of the dwelling fund administered by socialist organizations.

In the case of the lodgings mentioned in paragraph 1 and 2 above, the leases are contracted by tourist offices or the interested socialist organizations.

Art. 2. Natural persons domiciled in Romania are forbidden to accomodate such foreigners mentioned in Article 1, whether in the form of lease, sublease or the entertaining of guests, or to make places available to them for portable shelter.

Mature persons domiciled in Romania can provide lodgings in the living unit owned by them only to visiting foreigners who are close relatives, i.e., spouses, children, parents, and siblings, along with their spouses and children.

Art. 3. If contracted earlier with foreigners temporarily staying in Romania or with foreign juristic persons, the leases and subleases of living units owned by natural persons domiciled in Romania shall expire within 3 months from the date of promulgation of the present law-decree.

The executive committees of people's councils of counties and the municipality of Bucharest, in conjunction with the ministries and other central organs concerned, shall take measures for finding appropriate lodgings in hotels or other buildings under the management of socialist organizations, with a view to leasing them to foreign juristic and natural persons whose lease expires pursuant to the provision of paragraph 1 of this article.

Art. 4. Infringement of the provisions of Article 2, unless the act has been committed under circumstances qualifying it as a crime according to the law, constitutes a misdemeanor and shall be punished with a fine of 5,000 to 15,000 lei.

Misdemeanors shall be determined by agents of the executive committees of people's councils, by officers and junior officers of the Ministry of Interior, who shall levy the fine.

In the case of misdemeanors defined in paragraph 1, the provisions of Act 32/1968 on the determination and punishment of misdemeanors shall be applied.

Art. 5. The provisions of Article 17 of Act 5/1973 on the management of the dwelling fund and on the regulation of the relationship between owner and lessee, promulgated in Part I of *Monitorul Oficial* No. 47. dated March 31, 1973, furthermore the provisions of cabinet decision No. 862/1967 on the lease and sublease of certain lodgings in the possession of citizens for the accomodation of tourists, promulgated in Part 1 of *Monitorul Oficial* No. 34. dated April 20, 1967, as well as all other regulations running counter to the present law decree shall cease to have effect.

Bucharest, December 6, 1974.

(signed) Nicolae Ceausescu
President
of the Socialist Republic of Romania

(*Source: Monitorul Oficial,* Vol. X. No. 154, Part I, December 9, 1974.)

C

Modification of the Statute on the Accomodation of Foreigners

Law-decree No. 372/1976 of the State Council

modifying certain provisions of law-decree No. 184/1974 of the State Council on a surcharge applicable to the purchase and sale of foreign currency in connection with non-commercial operations, and of Law-decree No. 225/1974 of the State Council on the provision of lodging to foreigners temporarily staying in Romania.

The State Council of the Socialist Republic of Romania decrees:

(...)

IV. Article 2 of Law-decree No. 225/1974 of the State Council, transmuted into Act 89/1974, on the provision of lodging to foreigners temporarily staying in Romania is to be supplemented by the following text constituting Articles 3 and 4:

Accomodation may similarly be provided by any relatives domiciled in Romania:

(a) to persons of Romanian national origin who have acquired foreign citizenship or are stateless;

(b) to persons who have settled abroad and no longer have valid Romanian passports, but who have not renounced their Romanian citizenship;

(c) to spouses and kinfolk defined in paragraph 2 of the persons mentioned in subparagraphs (a) and (b) above.

Exceptionally, with the consent of the Ministry of Interior, accomodation may also be provided to other foreigners of Romanian descent.

Bucharest, November 8, 1976.

(signed) Nicolae Ceausescu
President
of the Socialist Republic of Romania

(*Source: Monitorul Oficial*, Vol. XII. No. 96, Part I, November 9, 1976)

D

Statute on the Liability of Romanian citizens to Refund Certain Expenses

Law-decree No. 402/1982 of the State Council

on the liability of persons who apply for permission to settle definitively abroad, and whose request has been granted, to repay in full debts owed to the state, to socialist organizations, and to natural persons, and to refund certain expenses incurred by the state in connection with their education.

Pursuant to the general political programme of party and state aimed at steadily raising the living standards of the entire population, considerable funds are allocated for the purpose of guaranteeing citizens of the country free education at all levels, free medical treatment, and a comprehensive system of social security and social welfare services.

With a view to having these expenditures refunded in accordance with the principles of socialist ethics and equity, it is necessary that persons permanently leaving the country compensate society for its outlays expended in the interest of their education and professional training, as well as for other services utilized prior to leaving the country.

For this purpose the State Council of the Socialist Republic of Romania decrees:

Art. 1. Persons requesting and obtaining permission to settle abroad permanently are responsible for the repayment of all debts owed to the state, to all social institutions and other organizations.

Art. 2. Those persons who have obtained permission to settle abroad must repay the Romanian state for their high school, college or university education in convertible currency. They are also liable for their studies toward the doctorate or other professional training for which they have received scholarship support or incurred other debts.

The debt owed will be determined on the basis of the laws of the Romanian Socialist Republic which regulate the tuition expenses of foreign students.

The present article is not applicable to those persons who have fulfilled their employment responsibilities and are of retirement age at the time when permission is granted for their settlement abroad.

Art. 3. The payment of these debts to the Romanian state, social institutions, as well as child support and other such responsibilities owed to natural persons, as well as all debts owed for education, professional training and on the job instruction, must be paid in full between the time that permission is granted for emigration and the issuance of a passport.

Art. 4. The persons belonging to the category mentioned in article 1, from the moment they receive permission to leave to the actual time of their departure, must pay all their medical expenses in convertible currency and are subject to costs and prices determined for tourists, and any other fees spelled out by the law of the Romanian Socialist Republic which regulate the stay of the foreigners who do not have established resident status in the country.

Art. 5. The properties, buildings and other real estate, belonging to persons who are leaving the country permanently, legally become the property of the state.

Art. 6. Those who have been granted permission to settle abroad permanently must also relinquish their art treasures and cultural possessions. They must turn these cultural possessions over to the state on the basis of the valuation established by the state's Central Committee on National Cultural Treasures.

Art. 7. Those persons who leave the country illegally, or those who travel abroad and do not return to the country by the required time limit, will have their properties confiscated by the state to assure payment for their education, professional preparation and the expenses of their job training. The legal seizure extends to both domestic and foreign properties owned, up to the limit owed the state.

Art. 8. The reimbursement for state expenditures mentioned in articles 2 and 4, including scholarships, as well as fees and other state incured expenses, must be paid by convertible currency either by bank transfer of funds or in person, in cash or by check.

Bucharest, November 1, 1982.

(signed) Nicolae Ceausescu

President
of the Socialist Republic of Romania

(Source: *Monitorul Oficial*, Vol. XVII, No. 95, Part I, November 1, 1982)

Name Index

Ara-Kovács, Attila xiii, 6, 56, 118
Babeş 47, 72, 115
Balas, Iolanda 98
Balogh, Edgár 50
Bartók, Béla 74
Báthory Family 109
Bolyai, János 47, 64, 72, 113, 115
Brezhnev, Leonid 116
Carol II, King of Romania 112
Ceausescu, Elena 119
Ceausescu, Nicolae xi-xiv, 3, 7, 39, 44, 49, 54, 59, 61, 76, 109, 116-119
Ciano, Galeazzo 62
Constantinescu, Miron 115
Costea, Aurel 51
Cuza, A.C. 89
Csendes, Zoltán 56
Danos, Miklós 72
Demeter, János 72
Demus, László 118
Domokos, Géza 50
Dózsa, György 74
Drondore, Grigore 72

Fazekas, János 51
Ford, Gerald 117
Gaál, Gábor 114
Gere, Mihály 51
Gheorghe, Lionte 102
Gheorghiu-Dej, Gheorghe 42, 113, 115-116
Ghere, Mihai (see Mihály Gere) 51
Gorbachev, Mikhail S. 118
Groza, Petru 41, 113
Gyárfás, Kurkó 42, 114
Hámos, László xiii, 117
Hitler, Adolf 62, 112
Horthy, Miklós Admiral, Regent of Hungary 111
Jakab, Antal 83
Jakabffy, Elemér 111
Jászi, Oszkár 110
Joó, Rudolf ix, xiii, xvi, 3
Kádár, János xi, xvii, 98, 115, 117
Kájoni 74
Kányádi, Sándor 73
Károlyi, Mihály 111

Khrushchev, Nikita 115
Király, Károly 51, 56, 117-118
Komocsin, Zoltán 116
Kós, Károly 111
Kossuth, Lajos 109
Kovacs, Iosif / József Kovács 72
Kun, Béla 111
Lancranjan, Ion 118
Lázár, György 56
Luka, Vasile 114
Maniu, Iuliu 40, 110, 113
Marina, Iustinian 79
Márton, Áron 83, 114
Mathias Rex/Mátyás Hunyadi, King of Hungary 110
Mikecs, László 64
Méliusz, József 50
Miłosz, Czesław 3
Mussolini, Benito 62
Pacepa, Ion Mihai 9, 56, 118
Pauker, Ana 114
Rab, István 51
Radescu, Nicolae 40
Rajk, László 47
Rákóczi Family 109

Rákóczi, György I 74
Rákosi, Mátyás 97
Ribbentrop, Joachim von 62
Ruha, Stefan 98
Sanatescu, Constantin 40
Stalin, Iosip V. 114-115
Stephen I, (Saint) King of Hungary 109
Sütő, András 50
Szabédi, László 56
Szász, József 51
Szentgyörgyi, István 76
Szőcs, Géza xiii, 15, 56, 104, 118
Szokai, Imre 100
Szűrös, Mátyás 100
Tabajdi, Csaba 100
Takáts, Lajos 56, 74
Tennant, Chris xviii
Tito, Josip Broz 114
Tőkés, László 119
Tóth, Antal Károly xiii, 56
Tóth, Károly 118
Tóth, Sándor 56
Trajan 23

Place Index

Alba (Fehér) county 35
Alba-Iulia (Gyulafehérvár) 81-86, 110-111, 114
Albania 49
Algeria 98
Arad 31, 69, 110
Arad county 94
Ardeal (see Siebenbürgen/Erdély/Transylvania) 23
Arcus (Árkos) 75
Austria 27, 96, 105
Austria-Hungary 110
Bacău (Bákó) county 29, 31, 64
Baia-Mare (Nagybánya) 69
Balkan xii, 49
Banat (Bánság) 22-23, 34, 82
Belgrade 105, 118
Bessarabia xii, 112
Bihor (Bihar) county 31, 35, 94
Brăila 81
Braşov (Brassó) 14, 33, 69
Bucharest 29, 31-32, 60-61, 71, 74-75, 79, 82, 116, 118-119
Buda 109
Budapest xi, 6, 20-21, 93, 95, 98, 105, 111
Bukovina xii, 64
Burgenland 27
Byzantine xii, 49
Carpathian basin xv, 64, 100, 110
Carpathians 30, 64-65, 82, 86
Central Europe ix, 49, 98
Chiurus (Csomakörös) 75
Cluj (Kolozs) county 31, 35
Cluj (Kolozsvár) 33, 44, 47, 56, 60-62, 64, 69, 72, 74-77, 88-89, 98, 112-115
Costa Rica 3
Covasna (Kovászna) county 31, 35, 51, 60, 65-66
Csanád 82
Csongrád county 94
Czechoslovakia xi, 27, 47, 111-112, 116
Debrecen 95, 117
Denmark 3, 96
Eastern Europe xvi, 4, 6, 18, 26, 98
Eastern Transylvania 115

Eger 82
Erdély (see Transylvania/Ardeal/Siebenbürgen) 23
Europe ix, 1, 13, 22, 24, 27, 49, 93
France 98
Germany 48, 96, 103, 112-113
Great Britain 96
Hajdú-Bihar county 94
Harghita (Hargita) county 31, 35, 51, 60, 65-66
Helsinki 97, 117-118
Hungary xi, xv-xvi, 7, 18, 22-24, 26-27, 31, 47-48, 50, 56, 61-63, 67, 73, 76, 81-82, 84, 87, 89, 91-99, 101-102, 104-108, 110-118
Iaşi 82
Iran 119
Ireland 96
Israel 11, 103
Italy 62, 96, 112
Lakitelek xv
Liechtenstein 3
Ludus (Ludas) 44
Lugoj (Lugos) 111
Luxembourg 3
Madrid 118
Miercurea Ciuc (Csíkszereda) 60

Moldavia xii, 29-30, 33, 55, 64, 82
Moscow xii, 115
Mureş (Maros) county 31, 35
Mureş-Maghiar Antonomous Region 44, 47, 115-116
New York City 117
North America 27
Northern Bukovina 112
Northern Hungary 109
Northern Transylvania 89
Oradea (Nagyvárad) 33, 60, 69, 74-75, 82, 84, 95, 115, 117
Partium (Crisana) 22-23, 82, 109
Poland xi, 3-4, 9-10, 112, 115
Potsdam 114
Romania xi-xiii, xvi-xx, 1-14, 22-23, 26-31, 33, 35-37, 39, 41-43, 45, 47-49, 51-52, 55-57, 59, 61-63, 66-67, 71, 73, 75-76, 81-82, 84-87, 89-96, 98, 101-108, 110-118
Sălaj (Szilágy) county 31
Sărmăs (Sármás) 44
Satu-Mare (Szatmár) county 31, 69, 81-82
Satu-Mare (Szatmárnémeti) 69, 75, 84

Sfîntu-Gheorghe (Sepsiszentgyörgy) 60, 75
Siebenbürgen (see Erdély/Transylvania/Ardeal) 23
Southern Transylvania 89
Soviet Union (see USSR) 7, 27, 113
Sweden 105
Timiş (Temes) county 94
Timişoara (Temesvár) 33, 69, 75, 82, 84, 106, 115, 119
Tîrgu Mureş (Marosvásárhely) 33, 44, 60-61, 64, 69, 71-72, 75, 98, 114-115
Transdanubia 109
Transylvania (see Erdély/Ardeal/Siebenbürgen) xi-xiii, xvi-xix, 6-7, 21-25, 27-36, 40, 42, 44, 47, 51-56, 60, 62, 64, 65-66, 68-70, 73-75, 80, 82-86, 88-91, 93, 97-99, 101-102, 104, 109-113, 115-118
Transylvanian Alps 23, 55
Trianon 29, 62, 101, 111, 114
Turnu-Severin 51
USA 117
USSR (see Soviet Union) 7, 112-113, 115-116
Vatican xvii, 30, 85
Vienna 25, 62 94, 118
Wallachia xii, 33, 55
Warsaw 115-116
Western Europe ix, 26-27
Yalta 113-114
Yugoslavia 27, 47, 102, 111, 114
Zalău (Zilah) 95

Volumes Published in
"Atlantic Studies on Society in Change"

No. 1 — *Tolerance and Movements of Religious Dissent in Eastern Europe.* Edited by Béla K. Király. 1977.

No. 2 — *The Habsburg Empire in World War I.* Edited by R. A. Kann. 1978

No. 3 — *The Mutual Effects of the Islamic and Judeo-Christian Worlds: The East European Pattern.* Edited by A. Ascher, T. Halasi-Kun, B. K. Király. 1979.

No. 4 — *Before Watergate: Problems of Corruption in American Society.* Edited by A. S. Eisenstadt, A. Hoogenboom, H. L. Trefousse. 1979.

No. 5 — *East Central European Perceptions of Early America.* Edited by B. K. Király and G. Barány. 1977.

No. 6 — *The Hungarian Revolution of 1956 in Retrospect.* Edited by B. K. Király and Paul Jónás. 1978.

No. 7 — *Brooklyn U.S.A.: Fourth Largest City in America.* Edited by Rita S. Miller. 1979.

No. 8 — *Prime Minister Gyula Andrássy's Influence on Habsburg Foreign Policy.* János Decsy. 1979.

No. 9 — *The Great Impeacher: A Political Biography of James M. Ashley.* Robert F. Horowitz. 1979.

No. 10 Vol. I* — *Special Topics and Generalizations on the Eighteenth and Nineteenth Century.* Edited by Béla K. Király and Gunther E. Rothenberg. 1979.

---

* Volumes Nos. I through XXXI refer to the series *War and Society in East and Central Europe.*

No. 11 Vol. II	*East Central European Society and War in the Pre-Revolutionary 18th-Century.* Edited by Gunther E. Rothenberg, Béla K. Király, and Peter F. Sugar. 1982.
No. 12 Vol. III	*From Hunyadi to Rákóczi: War and Society in Late Medieval and Early Modern Hungary.* Edited by János M. Bak and Béla K. Király. 1982.
No. 13 Vol. IV	*East Central European Society and War in the Era of Revolutions: 1775-1856.* Edited by B. K. Király. 1984.
No. 14 Vol. V	*Essays on World War I: Origins and Prisoners of War.* Edited by Samuel R. Williamson, Jr. and Peter Pastor. 1983.
No. 15 Vol. VI	*Essays on World War I: Total War and Peacemaking, A Case Study on Trianon.* Edited by B. K. Király, Peter Pastor, and Ivan Sanders. 1982.
No. 16 Vol. VII	*Army, Aristocracy, Monarchy: War, Society and Government in Austria, 1618-1780.* Edited by Thomas M. Barker. 1982.
No. 17 Vol. VIII	*The First Serbian Uprising 1804-1813.* Edited by Wayne S. Vucinich. 1982.
No. 18 Vol. IX	Czechoslovak Policy and the Hungarian Minority 1945-1948. Kálmán Janics. Edited by Stephen Borsody. 1982.
No. 19 Vol. X	*At the Brink of War and Peace: The Tito-Stalin Split in a Historic Perspective.* Edited by Wayne S. Vucinich. 1982.
No. 20	*Inflation Through the Ages: Economic, Social, Psychological and Historical Aspects.* Edited by Edward Marcus and Nathan Schmuckler. 1981.
No. 21	*Germany and America: Essays on Problems of International Relations and Immigration.* Edited by Hans L. Trefousse. 1980.
No. 22	*Brooklyn College: The First Half Century.* Murray M. Horowitz. 1981.

No. 23　　　*A New Deal for the World: Eleanor Roosevelt and American Foreign Policy.* Jason Berger. 1981.

No. 24　　　*The Legacy of Jewish Migration: 1881 and Its Impact.* Edited by David Berger. 1982.

No. 25　　　*The Road to Bellapais: Cypriot Exodus to Northern Cyprus.* Pierre Oberling. 1982.

No. 26　　　*New Hungarian Peasants: An East Central European Experience with Collectivization.* Edited by Marida Hollos and Béla C. Maday. 1983.

No. 27　　　*Germans in America: Aspects of German-American Relations in the Nineteenth Century.* Edited by Allen McCormick. 1983.

No. 28　　　*A Question of Empire: Leopold I and the War of Spanish Succession, 1701-1705.* Linda and Marsha Frey. 1983.

No. 29　　　*The Beginning of Cyrillic Printing — Cracow, 1491. From the Orthodox Past in Poland.* Szczepan K. Zimmer. Edited by Ludwik Krzyzanowski and Irene Nagurski. 1983.

No. 29a　　 *A Grand Ecole for the Grand Corps: The Recruitment and Training of the French Administration.* Thomas R. Osborne. 1983.

No. 30
Vol. XI　　*The First War between Socialist States: The Hungarian Revolution of 1956 and Its Impact.* Edited by Béla K. Király, Barbara Lotze, Nandor Dreisziger. 1984.

No. 31
Vol. XII　　*The Effects of World War I, The Uprooted: Hungarian Refugees and Their Impact on Hungary's Domestic Politics.* István Mócsy. 1983.

No. 32
Vol. XIII　 *The Effects of World War I: The Class War after the Great War: The Rise Of Communist Parties in East Central Europe, 1918-1921.* Edited by Ivo Banac. 1983.

No. 33 Vol. XIV	*The Crucial Decade: East Central European Society and National Defense, 1859-1870.* Edited by Béla K. Király. 1984.
No. 35 Vol. XVI	*Effects of World War I: War Communism in Hungary, 1919.* György Péteri. 1984.
No. 36 Vol. XVII	*Insurrections, Wars, and the Eastern Crisis in the 1870s.* Edited by B. K. Király and Gale Stokes. 1985.
No. 37 Vol. XVIII	*East Central European Society and the Balkan Wars, 1912-1913.* Edited by B. K. Király and Dimitrije Djordjevic. 1986.
No. 38 Vol. XIX	*East Central European Society in World War I.* Edited by B. K. Király and N. F. Dreisziger, Assistant Editor Albert A. Nofi. 1985.
No. 39 Vol. XX	*Revolutions and Interventions in Hungary and Its Neighbor States, 1918-1919.* Edited by Peter Pastor. 1988.
No. 40 Vol. XXI	*East Central European Society and War, 1750-1920. Bibliography and Historiography.* Complied and edited by László Alföldi. Pending.
No. 41 Vol. XXII	*Essays on East Central European Society and War, 1740-1920.* Edited by Stephen Fischer-Galati and Béla K. Király. 1988.
No. 42 Vol. XXIII	*East Central European Maritime Commerce and Naval Policies, 1789-1913.* Edited by Apostolos E. Vacalopoulos, Constantinos D. Svolopoulos, and Béla K. Király. 1988.
No. 43 Vol. XXIV	*Selections, Social Origins, Education and Training of East Central European Officers Corps.* Edited by Béla K. Király and Walter Scott Dillard. 1988.
No. 44 Vol. XXV	*East Central European War Leaders: Civilian and Military.* Edited by Béla K. Király and Albert Nofi. 1988.
No. 46	*Germany's International Monetary Policy and the European Monetary System.* Hugo Kaufmann. 1985.

No. 47	*Iran Since the Revolution — Internal Dynamics, Regional Conflicts and the Superpowers.* Edited by Barry M. Rosen. 1985.
No. 48 Vol. XXVII	*The Press During the Hungarian Revolution of 1848-1849.* Domokos Kosáry. 1986.
No. 49	*The Spanish Inquisition and the Inquisitional Mind.* Edited by Angel Alcala. 1987.
No. 50	*Catholics, the State and the European Radical Right, 1919-1945.* Edited by Richard Wolff and Jorg K. Hoensch. 1987.
No. 51 Vol. XXVIII	*The Boer War and Military Reforms.* Jay Stone and Erwin A. Schmidl. 1987.
No. 52	*Baron Joseph Eötvös, A Literary Biography.* Steven B. Várdy. 1987.
No. 53	*Towards the Renaissance of Puerto Rican Studies: Ethnic and Area Studies in University Education.* Maria Sanchez and Antonio M. Stevens. 1987.
No. 54	*The Brazilian Diamonds in Contracts, Contraband and Capital.* Harry Bernstein. 1987.
No. 55	*Christians, Jews and Other Worlds: Patterns of Conflict and Accommodation.* Edited by Phillip F. Gallagher. 1988.
No. 56 Vol. XXVI	*The Fall of the Medieval Kingdom of Hungary: Mohács, 1526, Buda, 1541.* Géza Perjés. 1989.
No. 57	*The Lord Mayor of Lisbon: The Portuguese Tribune of the People and His 24 Guilds.* Harry Bernstein. 1989.
No. 58	*Hungarian Statesmen of Destiny: 1860-1960.* Edited by Paul Bödy. 1989.
No. 59	*For China: The Memoirs of T. G. Li, former Major General in the Chinese Nationist Army. T. G. Li.* Written in collaboration with Roman Rome. 1989.

No. 60	*Politics in Hungary: For A Democratic Alternative.* János Kis, with an Introduction by Timothy Garton Ash. 1989.
No. 61	*Hungarian Worker's Councils in 1956.* Edited by Bill Lomax. 1990.
No. 62	*Essays on the Structure and Reform of Centrally Planned Economic Systems.* Paul Jonas. A joint publication with Corvina Kiadó, Budapest. 1990.
No. 63	*Kossuth as a Journalist in England.* Éva H. Haraszti. A joint publication with Akadémiai Kiadó, Budapest. 1990.
No. 64	*From Padua to the Trianon, 1918-1920.* Mária Ormos. A joint publication with Akadémiai Kiadó, Budapest. 1990.
No. 65	*Towns in Medieval Hungary.* Edited by László Gerevich. A joint publication with Akadémiai Kiadó, Budapest. 1990.
No. 66	*The Nationalities Problem in Transylvania, 1867-1940.* Sándor Bíró. 1992.
No. 67	*Hungarian Exiles and the Romanian National Movement, 1849-1867.* Béla Borsi-Kálmán. 1991.
No. 68	*The Hungarian Minority's Situation in Ceausescu's Romania.* Edited by Rudolf Joó and Andrew Ludanyi. 1994.
No. 69	*Democracy, Revolution, Self-Determination. Selected Writings.* István Bibó. Edited by Károly Nagy. 1991.
No. 70	*Trianon and the Protection of Minorities.* József Galántai. A joint publication with Corvina Kiadó, Budapest. 1991.
No. 71	*King Saint Stephen of Hungary.* György Györffy. A joint publication with Corvina Kiadó, Budapest. 1994.
No. 72	*Dynasty, Politics and Culture. Selected Essays.* Robert A. Kann. Edited by Stanley B. Winters. 1991.
No. 73	*Jadwiga of Anjou and the Rise of East Central Europe.* Oscar Halecki. Edited by Thaddeus V. Gromada. A joint

publication with the Polish Institute of Arts and Sciences of America, New York. 1991.

No. 74
Vol. XXIX
Hungarian Economy and Society During World War Two. Edited by György Lengyel. 1993.

No. 75
The Life of a Communist Revolutionary, Béla Kun. György Borsányi. 1993.

No. 76
Yugoslavia: The Process of Disintegration. Laslo Sekelj. 1993.

No. 77
Vol. XXX
Wartime American Plans for a New Hungary. Documents from the U.S. Department of State, 1942-1944. Edited by Ignác Romsics. 1992.

No. 78
Vol. XXXI
Planning for War against Russia and Serbia. Austro-Hungarian and German Military Strategies, 1871-1914. Graydon A. Tunstall, Jr. 1993.

No. 79
American Effects on Hungarian Imagination and Political Thought, 1559-1848. Géza Závodszky. 1994.